When the Universe Said Hello Back

When the Universe Said Hello Back

*Inspiring True Stories
of the Soul Sparking Moments
that Changed Our Lives*

Pakinam Fawal · Kelly Feeney
Kristina Green · Mandy McLaughlin
Deepika Sandhu

Foreword by Kathleen Cameron

Soul Sparks PRESS

soulsparkspress.com

ISBN 979-8-9922748-5-1 (paperback)
ISBN 979-8-9922748-6-8 (kindle)

Contents

Foreword

BY KATHLEEN CAMERON

When I was first invited to write this foreword for When The Universe Said Hello Back, I felt an overwhelming gratitude and connection. This book is not just a collection of stories, but a powerful reminder that the Universe is always speaking to, nudging, and guiding us. It is a testament to the subtle, magical ways our lives intertwine with divine messages and synchronicities, even when we are too busy or afraid to notice.

I believe in the power of "Soul Sparks"—those seemingly small but transformative moments when the Universe reaches out and taps us on the shoulder. These moments are whispers of truth, bursts of clarity, and sometimes, dramatic awakenings that force us to stop and listen. They are not coincidences, but profound invitations to embrace a more authentic and aligned version of ourselves.

Reflecting on my journey, I see a story deeply interwoven with the gentle yet profound nudges of the Universe. Like the authors in this book, I, too, have experienced Soul Sparks—those pivotal moments when the Universe whispers or even shouts, "You are not alone. Keep going. This is the way."

The stories in this book are living proof of these divine encounters. Each speaks to the courage to pause, reflect, and act when life feels unbearable or out of alignment. These authors share their journeys of heartbreak and healing, uncertainty and trust, fear and faith. They've faced moments when everything seemed to unravel, only to find that these moments were the beginning of something greater—an awakening, a transformation, a divine hello from the Universe itself.

As you turn these pages, I invite you to open your heart to the possibility that your life is filled with Soul Sparks. They may appear in the form of a kind stranger, a gentle breeze carrying a quiet message, or a deep inner knowing that you cannot ignore. They are here to remind you that you are never alone and that the Universe is always working in your favor, even when it feels like it is not.

May this book inspire you to slow down, tune in, and listen to the whispers of the Universe. May it remind you of your limitless potential and the divine guidance that is always available. And most importantly, may it spark something within you—a flicker of courage, a moment of clarity, a deep sense of trust—that propels you forward on your journey to becoming the best version of yourself.

Only Love,
Kathleen Cameron

Kathleen Cameron is the CEO & Founder of Diamond Academy. 8-figure manifestation coach, wealth creator, and best-selling author. Transformed a vision into a nearly $30M online empire in 4 years, harnessing the power of the law of attraction and manifestation. Empowering thousands globally to achieve unparalleled success and abundance.

Introduction

You are being nudged—slightly, subtly, and sometimes very obviously—by the Universe.

These nudges or whispers are the way the Universe speaks to you, guides you, and moves you along as you traverse this earthly terrain. It may be as subtle as a bird that grabs your attention while chirping and pecking outside your window or as obvious as slipping and falling before a big date (that guy is not for you... go home). It can be a confirmation to stay on the path you are on or it may be the push you needed to move in a different direction, one you have longed for but been too afraid to take.

I like to call these moments Soul Sparks.

Soul Sparks are the seemingly random, serendipitous and lovely moments that appear in your regular day to day life exactly when you need them. It is an occurrence that stops you in your tracks, makes you sit up, pause and take notice. It is a happening that ignites a subtle flicker, a tap, a touch, a glow on the deepest parts of yourself. A Soul Spark feels like, and is, indeed, a sign from the Universe, the Divine, God, the Holy Spirit, whatever you believe in (or don't believe) that is orchestrating this life.

It is not random.

It is not a coincidence.

It is the Universe's way of putting up a flare to get your attention.

The moment the Soul Spark appears in your life, you are lit from the inside. You are ignited by a sudden and profound thought or sensation. You feel it from deep within. It comes to you and opens you up in a way that you haven't felt before. It may last only a few seconds or it may change the trajectory of your life forever.

The feeling a Soul Spark creates within me is like the first sip of my Nani's chai. My Grandma made the best chai. She would place the pot of water on the stove, splash in some milk and sprinkle in the cardamom and the cinnamon. She would let the pot slowly come up to a boil, then down to a simmer, then up to a boil again, until the color of her chai was just the perfect shade of brown. The aromatic dance of these special spices tickled my nose, awakened my senses and brought a smile to my face. I could not wait to get the perfectly sized tea cup into my hand. The first sip was always magical. The warmth of the tea would touch my lips, slip down my throat, and reach all parts of my body, warming it all along the way. With that first sip, I was so aware, so present, so in the moment, of the chai and all of its sensations.

The same happens with a Soul Spark. When you recognize that one has appeared, you feel it. You are aware of it. You are present with it. You just know there is more to this little moment than meets the eye.

Your life is filled with them.

Mine certainly is.

Yet, for most of my life, I was so caught up in my own day to day preoccupations that I could hardly see them. If I did notice something that felt like a sign from the Universe, I was far more likely to dismiss it as a random coincidence. It wasn't until I started to put the brakes on my life that I began to see all the ways the world was speaking to me.

I was one of those women who wore her busyness as a badge of honor. I was rushing my way through life. Rushing to get ready each morning. Rushing to work. Rushing my way through meetings. Rushing home each day to be with my daughter. Rushing through dinner. Rushing through feeding my daughter. Rushing through bathing her. Rushing to read her a book. Rushing to put her to sleep so I could get back online and keep on working. All so I could go to bed late and wake up early and rush through it all again.

Of course, I only posted smiling, happy pictures on social media to make my life look exceedingly glamorous, effortless and anything but rushed. All the other working Mommas on social media, TV, and in the movies were juggling the same things and making it look so easy. I should too, right?

Yet, if I ever did stumble upon a moment of quiet while taking a walk or sitting in my backyard, I could literally hear my exhausted self ask: Why doesn't this feel right?

My life sent messages for a long time. I just didn't notice them. The man that stopped me in my tracks as I raced to work to give me a compliment—that was a Soul Spark. The fluffy dog with loving eyes that crossed my path on my evening walk, that was a Soul Spark. Even that feeling in my gut when I did something that made me feel alive. That was a Soul Spark too.

For the fleeting seconds when these instances occurred, I sensed someone or something was trying to catch my attention. But I just ignored it. I didn't pay it any mind. I let the compliment come and go. I pet the dog for a second and continued on my walk. I did the activity that lit me up and then never did it again. I just went back to the motions of my life with blinders on, not really seeing all that was going on around me.

But when I decided to slow my life down and became slightly less busy, slightly less scheduled, slightly less rushed, I started to see things in my everyday life that I never saw before.

Take the day I was walking through a crowded sidewalk in San Francisco. It was my regular path from the train station to my office and as usual it was overflowing with people. All of them walking with purposeful speed to their destination. Some with a coffee cup in hand. Others, texting away. A few weeks ago, I would have been like everyone else on this street.

Not today.

Today I was just watching the commotion of the morning as an observer rather than a participant. As I walked, a single pink flower petal fluttered in front of me, just hanging in the air as it slowly danced to the ground near my feet. Normally, I would have stomped on it and kept going or not have noticed it at all. But on this day, I not only saw it, I also took notice of it. Where did a flower petal even come from in the middle of this concrete jungle? And how did it land right in my line of sight? And how lovely to have these few seconds to observe this beautiful petal in the midst of this morning rush?

This too was a Soul Spark. It was a subtle and gentle confirmation that this newer, slower pace of life was suiting me. Letting go of the unnecessary busyness, the self-created hustle, the excess parties, people and activities that were consuming my life, was slowly creating a sliver of space for more. It was a reminder to be here, in the now, the present moment. To see the beauty of this life that I only noticed for fleeting seconds before.

But it is just a flower petal, you say. Why would a flower petal convey a message to you? Isn't that flower petal in your way just a coincidence?

That petal floating in my ethos as I was embracing a slower pace of life, just like so many other such moments, was not a coincidence. They were the shooting star in my day that changed the course I was on. They were a spark that touched deep within my soul. It was the tiny little nudge, hint, reassuring hug I needed to keep moving forward.

It was the moment the Universe said Hello Back.

This book brings you five beautiful Soul Sparking stories. The moment these women realized life needed to change. The moment they knew the Universe was working hard to get their attention because it was time.

Time for a different way.

Time for a different path.

Time to see more for themselves.

Time to stop being in the passenger seat in this life but to wake up, take notice and steer this life in the direction they desired and deserved.

They did not always know the way.

They did not know what would happen next.

Yet they got the Soul Spark, and they just knew life was not going to be the same.

And it wasn't.

For each of them, they went from their rock bottom moments– lying in a pile of dog piss after falling off a ladder while taking ornaments off the Christmas Tree; seeing the face of infidelity in the form of a new born child; the cold, dead body of their spouse in a hospital room; sitting for an interview with shingles all over her back; or even being rejected once again by the man she thought she loved–to realizing that their lives were going to be more than this. Far more. They were not going to be forever defined by the lowest of the lows. No. They were going to live a life where they rose up against what was happening to them to create into existence a life that was happening for them.

These are the stories we share with you today.

So, you can see every way the Universe is saying hello back to you.

You Are Beautiful

BY DEEPIKA SANDHU

"You are so beautiful."

I looked up, dumbfounded, wiping away the tears that were still streaming down my cheek.

Walking from my boyfriend's apartment to my car after another fight, I felt anything but beautiful. It was our typical fight. Not a shouting, yelling type of fight. In the year that we dated, we didn't have those. We had the type of fight where I would get bothered about something here and there but instead of bringing it up in the moment, I would just bottle it up inside until one day, it all came hurling out with forceful emotion, usually at a time when he was not expecting it.

I told him I was done. That we were over.

I sobbed, hoping he would console me, tell me it would all be okay, that he would change, that he wanted to be with me and we would make it work.

But he didn't say that. Instead, he said what he always said when I got upset. He just looked at me like he didn't care at all. Shrugged his shoulders. Gave a smirk like he was too good for this conversation and said I was being dramatic. He asked, "What's the big deal?" He wasn't taking me seriously. Had he ever taken me seriously?

I got up and walked out.

As I approached my car, a tall Scandinavian-looking woman with platinum blonde shoulder length hair was walking toward me.

She was stunningly gorgeous and perfectly dressed for the hot summer day. She radiated effortless beauty in a flowing, sleeveless, magenta top, skinny white pants, tan stilettos, and a designer handbag over her arm.

She was gorgeous.

"You are so beautiful."

She said it again.

I looked at her, confused.

Why was she calling *me* beautiful?

Her blue eyes were piercing.

Her smile was sincere.

Her energy was captivating.

I was mesmerized.

I did not feel beautiful at that moment. My eyes were puffy from all the crying. My heart was heavy for trying to make a man love me. My mind was questioning every action and inaction I took since meeting him. And then started my inner saboteur, that voice within that decided it was a good time to start critiquing my own appearance. How could I ever even think that I was desirable to a man? That was quickly followed by a litany of reasons I would never find another one. All of this in the few minutes it took me to walk to my car.

Yet here was this captivating, alluring, and gorgeous woman crossing my path complimenting *me*?

I stopped, I looked back at her, and mustered a tiny, forced smile.

Hesitantly, I met her gaze and said "Thank you."

Her simple words, her compliment, her smile, her effortlessness, were not just spoken by one passerby to the other.

They transcended my entire physical being and landed on my soul.

It wasn't just a compliment.

Her words were the exact message I needed to hear.

I needed to know that I was beautiful.

I needed to know my own self-worth.

I needed to know that I was better than this relationship.

I needed to know that I was loveable.

I needed to know that so much more was possible for me.

In her simple compliment, she transported that message right to my soul.

I heard it.

I felt it.

I will never forget it.

Why?

Because it was a Soul Spark.

It was not random.

It was not a coincidence.

It was the Universe's way of putting up a flare to get my attention.

This woman calling me beautiful definitely did that. For over a year, I was in a relationship with this man, who did not love me and probably was never capable of loving me. He certainly was not going to love me the way I wanted, needed or deserved to be loved. The longer I was with him, the less beautiful, attractive and desirable I felt. In his own subtle ways, he slowly, yet repeatedly, rejected me more and more each day. And I let him. Over and over again. I not only tolerated but accepted these behaviors.

The Universe wanted me to stop.

I am sure the Universe previously presented other subtle hints that I did not recognize or respond to. I was too wrapped up in getting this guy to love me to see whatever hints were being dropped.

But now with this woman who appeared before me as an authority on all things beauty the Universe decided to not be so subtle. It didn't deliver a Soul Spark but a giant inferno. It wanted to get my attention. And it did.

It wasn't the first time that I received a compliment. People had made nice comments about my appearance before. But I was always quick to dismiss them. I did not believe it to be true. "Oh, they are just being nice," I would think to myself. Never did I believe they were giving me their genuine opinion. Maybe I could not fully receive those compliments about me in the past because I did not believe them about myself.

This hit different.

Hearing that I am beautiful from such a captivating and alluring woman made me sit up and take notice. It made me realize how little I was valuing myself in this relationship. It made me realize that I was capable of being with someone who would recognize my own beauty and self-worth. It made me realize that I needed to see the beauty within me before anyone else would.

But I didn't listen to that spark.

Despite that Soul Spark being loud, clear, stopping me in my tracks, shaking me, speaking to me in the core of my being, I didn't listen.

That boyfriend whose house I left in tears, the one that I looked straight in the eye and said, "We are done! Don't contact me ever again!," the one who smirked at me, wondering what the big deal was - I ended up marrying that guy.

And I stayed married to that guy for 7 years, 4 months and 10 days. From the first date to signed divorce papers was 12 years, 8 months and 26 days. But hey, who is counting?

You know what I should have kept count of? The number of Soul Sparks that came from the minute we got back together, the time we were engaged and all the years we were married. Countless.

The Soul Sparks came in droves. Each one tried to get my attention. But I ignored them. Every single one. Just like the captivatingly gorgeous women telling me I am beautiful, the Soul Sparks came, they tried so hard to wake me up and see the light. And I did. Sometimes for a couple of weeks. In a few cases, even a couple of months. But each and every time, the Soul Spark, no matter how clear, no matter how profound, came and went.

I willingly, knowingly, consciously, continuously ignored them. Instead of listening, I continuously played small. Shrinking myself more and more to contort, however uncomfortable it may be, into smaller and smaller versions of myself that could fit into this relationship which eventually turned into a marriage. Day after day, year after year, it was the same. Trying to make something work that did not feel right to me in any way.

Why?

I suppose I could say the story was meant to go this way. That had I not ignored all those Soul Sparks along the way, I may have never gotten married, I may never have had my daughter, I may never have had the experiences that led me to write books, create a publishing company and live the abundant life I enjoy today.

But that isn't it.

I ignored the soul sparks because of fear. I was afraid of them.

The beautiful woman telling me I am beautiful. Maybe she was wrong? Maybe she was just being nice? Maybe I am not that beautiful? Maybe I should just take what I can get?

The boyfriend turned husband smirking and saying "What's the big deal?" Maybe he was right? Maybe it wasn't a big deal? Maybe I was blowing it out of proportion.

The times in the marriage when he would make me feel small, mock me in front of his friends, when I didn't feel accepted by him or them and he would dismiss it and paint me to be the unfriendly one? Maybe he was right? Was this all just silly banter? Maybe I should take it lightly? Maybe I was the unfriendly one?

Each and every time a Soul Spark landed in my life, each time I had the feeling that something was not right, that I did not want to live this way, that things could or should be better, I dismissed the sensation. I might have considered it for a few minutes, a few hours, maybe even a few days. But each and every time I just returned to how things were.

I was simply too afraid. Too afraid to trust that making a change in my life might lead to a better outcome for me. Too scared to trust the messages I was hearing and feeling. Too insecure to believe things could be different. Instead, I kept everything the same.

Sure, there might be drama some days. Days where I threatened to leave him. Not speaking to one another for days on end. Booking a trip with girlfriends to get away from the situation. Drinking a bit too much wine as a means of avoiding what needed to be dealt with. Even creating a fantasy land with George Clooney as my alternative leading man, because, hey, why not?

The problem with the drama, the avoidance tactics, the fantasies, was that nothing ever changed. Not because it couldn't–but because I wouldn't let it.

I was too afraid to ever fully embrace and move towards the change I knew in my gut I needed to make because I was too scared. What was familiar to me—no matter how much I disliked it, no matter how much I cried over it, no matter how much I dreamed of something different—was comfortable. I knew how to exist in the world that I created. I had no idea how to exist in a world that didn't have this husband, this house, this life.

Until I met Diane.

Diane was a psychic with a PhD, a strong southern accent, and ended almost every sentence with "that's what I am talking about!" She was scattered, a bit disorganized, but spoke directly to my spirit with her riveting insights. She was one of many healers, astrologers and mystics that started to make their way into my world when the day to day of my marriage was becoming too much to bear. I did not seek out this cast of characters. Far from it. But as my life was thrown further into chaos, stress and sadness, the Universe started to present people in various forms that were going to help me see another way.

And boy did she.

She could see parts of myself that I could not see or was unwilling to acknowledge. She saw beneath the armor of a high-powered career woman, who seemingly had it all, but was feeling empty and depleted on the inside. She illuminated with perfect accuracy the challenges in my life. She knew that I needed to make big changes to not just get out of the situation I was in but to move fully into my soul's purpose.

We spoke for months. Each time she added another nugget that perfectly resonated. I wanted to believe everything she said but my logical self resisted. My inner critic–the voice within that had a front row seat to my life and would question every differing thought I had, especially when I was trying something new–would berate me for talking to her in the first place. But as my life continued to feel terribly off course, as the desperation kicked in, I could not help but wonder if all she was saying was true.

Was there another love waiting for me as she said to me countless times?

Was I going to launch something new, kick off a new cycle in my life, the minute I separated from my husband's energy?

Was my fear of losing money in divorce just fleeting because so much more abundance and prosperity was coming my way?

I listened and listened. I got glimmers of hope each time. But within minutes of our conversations ending, I would doubt again. The questions would flood my mind and overwhelm me.

How could this happen?

How could I leave him?

My family won't understand!

People will judge me!

Friends will call my seemingly perfect life a fraud.

Oh, forget the friends.

What about my daughter?

Am I ruining her life forever?

How would I manage as a single mom?

Will I lose my money?

Will I lose my house?

Where would we live?

How will I do life all alone?

The fear was so deeply rooted. No matter what I may read in a spiritual book, see on an inspiring Instagram post or even hear directly from such a kind-hearted and intuitive soul like Diane, my doubts were on overdrive. If I couldn't see the path from where I was right now to where I wanted to be, I couldn't make even the tiniest of moves in that direction. I mean, how could I? I spent my entire life needing a plan and living with a checklist. I knew how to navigate doing well in college. I knew how to navigate the corporate world to get promotions, another raise and more accolades. None of that required anything else than hard work and determination. If I put in the effort at school or work I would always get the result. I knew that to be true because it was proven to me in real life over and over again.

How could I just operate on faith, trust and belief now? Even if I wanted to, I did not know how. I had no tools at my disposal other than what Diane was telling me. And honestly, at some level I wondered if I should even be listening to a disorganized psychic from the deep South. The optics of this seemed crazy even though everything she said resonated in the deepest parts of my soul.

I knew how deeply I wanted out of this marriage. I recognized so clearly all the ways this marriage was not aligned to the real me. All the ways it was keeping me stuck, trapped, stagnant. I was seeing the signs, getting the insights, and just knew. Yet I still was paralyzed from doing anything about it.

During one of our many conversations, I told Diane that I couldn't see the path from the life I lived to what she was predicting. She then said something that put my thinking mind in a tizzy but reverberated so deeply with my deepening spiritual senses. She said *"Honey, it don't matter if you can't see it. The Universe is pushing this rock up the hill and it's 'bout to come down the other side and ain't nothing you gonna be able to do about it."*

She was right.

After years and years of Soul Sparks, after desperate attempts by the Universe to catch my attention, after me willfully ignoring it all (sometimes after much thought and mental gymnastics), the Universe took the decision into its own hands.

It knew I would never leave my husband. Despite giving me every opportunity to exit my situation, every nudge, every cosmic push,

I exercised my own free will and stayed put. I was simply too afraid of what would happen if I did. Not because of what he might do. I wasn't afraid of him. I was afraid of stepping into the unknown of a new life.

But after years and years of succumbing to that fear, the Universe had enough. It knew what I was unwilling to accept. That the grandest version of who I am meant to become could only emerge by not being in this marriage. It knew I was strong enough to handle what was coming. So, it put into motion all the steps that made it my reality. Including a big burly dude pounding on my windows at 7 a.m. on a Saturday morning to serve me with divorce papers.

I was feeding my daughter breakfast. My husband said he needed to leave the house super early for some work. That had never happened before, particularly this early on a Saturday morning but I didn't make much of it. More time for just me and my daughter to enjoy. We were in our usual routine of silly kid talk while eating breakfast. As I was sipping my coffee, I heard a loud and jarring thud on our windows. No one had ever pounded on our windows before. I jumped from the breakfast table startled. Was someone trying to break in? Who would break into our home at 7 a.m. in broad daylight? I carefully walked to the door, looked through the peephole to see a man looking directly into the peephole waving a manila envelope. He kept pounding and shouting "OPEN THE DOOR." I was shaking. Completely unsure of what to do, I opened the door just slightly. The man looked me dead in the eye, dropped the envelope at my feet and shouted "YOU HAVE BEEN SERVED!"

I stood still as I watched him walk back to his car and race off. I slowly reached for the envelope, took it in both hands, and stared at it for what felt like forever. I did not know what it was but I knew it was about to change everything. With the sound of the man's fists pounding on my windows still ringing in my head, I closed the door and walked back to the kitchen to my daughter's startled face. Even her three-year-old self knew something was wrong.

But maybe it was all unfolding exactly as it needed to.

I did not see it playing out like this. On the days when I could visualize a new life, when I would pray for things to be different, when I would cry myself to sleep asking God to show me the way, I had no inkling that it would go down like this. That he would file for divorce, that he would send a big burly dude to the home we both shared with each other and our daughter, that I would be served with divorce papers.

I spent so many years carefully curating a life that seemed perfect from the outside. A happy family. A beautiful house. Nice cars. Fabulous vacations. Loads of smiles posted on social media for all to see.

Now with this one move, that I didn't see coming, that perfectly curated life would burn in an inferno of lengthy divorce proceedings, lies, arguments, trickery, pain, shame, anger, frustration and brutal sadness.

But, Universe had to take the wheel just like Diane predicted.

Afterall, I had already ignored 10 years of Soul Sparks. Each one slowly chipped away at my own awareness, helping me to see that this life I created was not the life that I wanted or needed. Each one helped me see that more was meant for me. But how to make the changes to get out of this life and into that new life, that I could not do. Not even a little bit. I was paralyzed.

This move by the Universe changed that. Just as Dianne said, the Universe moved the rock up the hill one Soul Spark at the time, waiting for me to be brave enough, courageous enough, strong enough to do what needed to be done. But when it saw that I would not do it, it took control and pushed things into motion for me.

Being served divorce papers was devastating and shocking. But the more I sat with it, the more I realized it was a gift. Universe worked through him to bring a situation to a head for the betterment of both of us. And for that I am profoundly grateful.

But should I have waited for the Universe to take over?

Hmmm.

Should I have listened to the countless soul sparks that were nudging me, guiding me, employing me to make a change?

Maybe.

Should I have caught on when that gorgeous Scandinavian woman delivered one of the most soul stirring Soul Sparks of my life?

Probably.

Rather than beat myself up and wonder why I wasn't smarter, did not catch on sooner, and wasted so much time, I came to a profound realization instead.

We only get the awareness when we are ready to receive it.

The Universe was busy telling me it was here, that it was with me, trying to show me a different way. But the true path, the step I was meant to take, the experience I needed to trudge through to see a new way, could only emerge when I was ready for it.

The problem was I did not know I was ready. But the Universe sure did.

My husband initiating the divorce was the Universe confirming to me in every possible way that I could handle all that would come next. Left to my own accord, I didn't believe I was ready to walk out, to leave him, to find a new place, to start over. Sure, I thought about it. Deep down in my bones, I knew it was what I needed. But I simply lacked the courage to take the action. That fear kept me in the hamster wheel of simply existing within a life that was no longer serving me.

The Universe did not want that to persist any longer. It took control.

Yes, being served divorce papers felt like a punch in the gut. Yes, I was surprised, even shocked. I never thought he had it in him to want to leave me. But in that moment, amidst the shock and surprise, I did not shed a tear. I did not scream and question why. I did not beg him to stay, to withdraw the divorce petition, to not give my daughter a broken home. Nope. I did not do any of that.

In that moment I accepted and surrendered to what was happening.

The awareness was coming bit by bit. It was preparing me, encouraging me, moving me toward action. My own free will and self-determination kept me there, physically. But internally, I was growing, I was evolving, I was becoming the woman who absolutely could handle what was coming her way.

AND I DID.

This is how I learned awareness is the Universe in action.

At the time the divorce started, I was fully aware I would be okay. That divorce was the answer. I understood that from the depths of myself. The situations, circumstances, and even the people like Dianne that showed up in my life, were confirming that every single day.

But, with the awareness must come the action to make what we are becoming aware of our lived reality. We must take it from the awareness in our minds and cement it in our lives. We must give it the chance and space to be present, here, in the physical reality and not just a wish, a hope, a desire.

The Universe wants us to seek good for ourselves but it also requires us to do something to make it happen. We cannot sit on the sidelines and only hope and pray for a different way. Perhaps that is an option for a while. But that hoping and praying alone is the slowest possible route to what you desire. Just like it plants the seeds of what it is you need to do, the Universe also clearly shows you the path to that result. It will show you the action. It will show you the movement that is required. You will get the awareness. You will receive it. But to move into action requires faith.

Profound complete and total faith.

The problem was, I had no faith.

The Universe waited patiently for me to spring into action of my own volition. But I lacked the belief in myself to move from what I knew so clearly in my mind to the aligned actions that would shape my reality for the better. The act of being served divorce papers is what moved me into faith. My immediate response to it all was not to scream, to cry, to be upset, to think that life was over, to have fear of what the divorce journey would be like. No, none of that. Instead, I stepped into faith in a way that I have never done before. My simple mantra was "Universe, show me the way." If you decided to take the wheel, if you decided I was ready, then I now know fully, deeply, and completely in every part of me, that I must have profound faith to move into what is truly meant for me.

I would repeat this mantra countless times every day. Every time it got uncomfortable. Every time I wavered. Every time fear would emerge. I repeated this mantra. I would cry myself to sleep with this mantra. I would wake up in the middle of the night with my stomach in knots, I would repeat this mantra. I repeated and repeated and repeated it until they were no longer words that I recited, but a truth I embodied, a belief that was overtaking every inch of my being.

Each step of this divorce journey could have crushed my faith. After all, it was the most difficult experience of my life. It left me broke, heartbroken, exhausted. But it did not destroy my faith. I knew each step was leading me towards the version of myself that I was meant to become.

And it did.

Now there are days where the beauty of this life overwhelms me. My daughter and I are thriving in our happy home living our extraordinary ordinary life. Loving the simple and beautiful moments of singing along to Taylor Swift in the car, walking our dog in the evenings, and even binge watching a new show together snuggled up on the couch. There is joy in seeing her grow up with two happy parents in their respective homes. She is watching her momma do big things and be the very best version of herself, so she can learn to be her best version too. All of it is what I knew I wanted and now, through faith, through action, through a belief that it can all be better, it is beyond better.

I am in wonderment of all that *is* in our lives today.

The beauty in knowing, and no longer seeking.

The strength of operating in faith, and no longer the weakness of fear.

The awareness of each moment, and no longer the constant questioning of doubt.

Believing with loving curiosity in all that is and the profound knowingness that it is always, always, always working out for me.

Trusting ALL OF IT because I know...

This life is beautiful.

Deepika is the CEO of Soul Sparks Press, a six-time award-winning, best-selling author, TV show host, retired Silicon Valley Business Executive, and Mom. Deepika has inspired more than 20,000 people worldwide through her books, speaking, thought leadership, courses, and one-on-one private mentorship. Deepika's debut book *Hello Universe, It's Me* garnered literary acclaim as a 2024 Critically Acclaimed Best Seller by the LA Tribune and as the winner of the 2023 Silver Prize at the Nautilus Book Awards.

Deepika lives in the San Francisco Bay Area with her sweet and sassy pre-teen daughter and their puppy.

Connect with Deepika on Instagram @deepikasandhu.co or at Soul Sparks Press soulsparkspress.com

The Colors of Grief

BY PAKINAM (PAKI) FAWAL

Have you ever had a moment when you knew, with absolute certainty, that your life would never be the same? For me, it was a Wednesday in June 2007 when my world collapsed and shattered.

I had always been someone who loved life, dressing in bright colors that matched my vibrant spirit. At work, my nickname was the school's butterfly. The thought of a colorless existence had never crossed my mind.

That evening, after a long day of proctoring and grading finals, I laid on my bed, hoping for a quick power nap. My husband had just left to play basketball, my mom had taken my youngest child, and my oldest was with me at home.

About an hour had passed when the calm of the moment was interrupted by a ringing phone. One of our closest friends, Dr. Omar called, sounding tense, to tell me my husband, Tarek, had an incident while playing and was now in the hospital. He said he was coming to pick me up.

I remember vividly that I was wearing a red T-shirt and beige shorts.

As I glanced at myself in the mirror, a chilling thought flashed through my mind: would I be destined to wear black from now on?

Dr. Omar was playing basketball with Tarek that day. When he arrived at our house, he insisted on leaving my son at his home with his wife and kids before heading to the hospital to see my husband. This unusual request filled my heart with worry. Something was terribly wrong, but I could not quite comprehend it, or maybe I was avoiding the inevitable. The unease troubled me. I couldn't help but wonder why Omar was coming to pick me up instead of Tarek calling me, or simply asking me to drive to the hospital.

As we dropped my son off at Omar's house, I noticed the somber expression on his wife's face as she held a black top in her hands.

My heart tightened, I tried to push away the growing sense of dread, desperately holding onto denial.

During the drive to the hospital, I bombarded our friend with all sorts of questions. His responses were short and strained, which only fueled my anxiety.

"What happened?" I asked.

"We were playing, and he did not feel well. He felt dizzy, so we took him to the hospital." He said.

His voice cracked under the weight of stress and emotion. As I kept asking clarifying questions, he finally snapped, which was unusual, "You'll see when we get there. You'll see!"

Upon arriving at the hospital, the cold sterility of the emergency room sent a chill through me. The ER doctor approached, his face full of sorrow and concern, and led me to a small room. With trembling hands, he handed me my husband's ring and wallet.

"We did the best we could. I'm sorry, we couldn't save him," the doctor said.

The words echoed in my mind, a cruel refrain that refused to make sense.

My mind in shock, I shook my head and both my hands signaling refusal, my heart was pounding fast and my breathing became heavy and loud.

"No, no, no... He's going to get those items himself! I'm not taking those, no, no, NO!" I cried.

My vibrant world, once filled with color and life, was now an all-encompassing blackness, fear, and denial.

THE LONG CORRIDOR

"I want to see him," I said.

"Let me see him," I repeated.

My husband's cousin, a physician at this hospital, offered to take me to the room where Tarek was kept.

I remember that corridor! It felt so long, dark, and cold.

I felt like I was being taken to my execution. I was moving one step forward and one step back, as if I was being dragged.

And... I saw him.

There he was laying back peacefully as if he was sleeping.

I touched his hand, and then his face.

His skin was still warm, deceiving me for a moment into thinking he might be alive but just sleeping.

At this moment, my body and my mind started shutting down. I was told later that I was given a shot because I was breathing really hard and lost consciousness. I do not remember anything else that happened at the hospital afterwards.

THE FURNITURE THAT SPOKE

When I got home, I had no idea what had happened to me.

There was furniture being moved around. The couches seemed to be talking to me: Where are you taking me? What is changing? What is going on?

I started to hear words like tragedy, gone, poor kids, young wife, what is she going to do?

Was the furniture talking? Was it these people talking? Where did these people come from? And suddenly, the sounds the furniture was making, their voices, seemed to get louder and louder and louder until I had to shut my ears.

I don't know whether it was something inside of me that was protesting this turn of events.

I don't know whether the furniture was speaking to my emotions.

I don't know what was happening and why I felt so disoriented.

I just knew I had to leave that space.

But where would I go?

My sons!

I had to find my sons!

They must be looking for me, they must be wanting their mother and honestly at that moment I wanted to be nothing more than a soothing mother to my grieving boys. I had to find my sons.

While I was looking for my two boys, I didn't know how their grief was unfolding.

I saw them.

Their innocent faces didn't fully understand the loss, but they were a small comfort.

I gathered them into my arms, and hugged their small warm and alive bodies.

In that moment, I felt an intense need to protect them, to shield them from the pain and confusion that would come. I held them tightly, trying to hold on to a piece of my husband and our life together.

Until today, my eldest son, 7-years-old at the time, tells me how confused he was when he was told by a relative that his father traveled to Australia to get medical treatment. Maybe that relative thought they were helping by creating a story of why his Dad was missing rather than explaining that he died. It did not help him, or me to hear this!

And I still cannot forget the cries of my youngest son, just 3-years-old, who had no idea how to comprehend that his father was gone, or what that even really meant. But he would wake up at midnight crying and asking for his father. His cries left me hollow and broken.

THE WEIGHT OF CULTURAL EXPECTATIONS

In our culture, it is a tradition for family and friends to flood the home of those who have lost a loved one, especially when tragedy strikes as it did in mine, with a young, healthy husband taken too soon, leaving behind a young grieving wife and two very young children.

Despite the well-meaning visits, the offers of help, and the crowded rooms, I felt an unbearable loneliness. The noise around me only amplified the silence within. I felt a void so deep that it threatened to swallow me. I was weak, broken, and lost in a roller coaster of emotions.

Some days, anger surged through me, anger at the world, at fate, at the cruel hand I had been dealt. I wanted to defy every rule, every tradition that dictated how I should grieve.

Other times, jealousy nibbled at my heart as I watched other families continue their lives untouched by tragedy.

I did not choose this path, and I had no way out.

Countless nights, sleep eluded me. Darkness became my tormentor, the silence amplifying the relentless replay of memories and 'what ifs' that haunted my waking hours.

GOLDEN HEARTS IN DARK TIMES

But in the midst of this darkness, something unexpected happened. I began to see people for who they really were.

I clearly remember the day my husband's body was taken from our home.

The sorrow was so heavy, I could barely breathe.

Yet, in that suffocating moment, a university friend of mine, someone I was not even particularly close to at that time, showed up. She had three boys who attended the same school as my sons, and without hesitation, she offered, as she had already planned, to take my children for the day, to give them a respite from the grief that filled our home. She wanted to shield them from the immediate chaos and grief that had engulfed our home. She shielded them from the tears, from the pain, from the harsh reality of what was happening.

In that act of kindness, her heart of gold shone brighter than anything I was able to see at the moment. In the midst of that darkness, I saw my friend's true heart.

It was in this moment of crisis that I realized—we truly understand the value of friends not just in times of joy, but in the darkest hours when we need them the most. That is when they show up, when they shine. The true value of friendship and humanity appears. I even started thinking about my relations with other people and friends. We need each other in the darkest times much more than in the happiest moments.

In my despair, I was deeply grateful to discover that I was surrounded by a handful of golden-hearted friends who stepped forward when it mattered most. I was blessed to have a handful of such golden friends, and yet, no one shone brighter than my parents. My mother, who had just submitted her retirement papers to finally join my father abroad, threw everything aside to stay with me.

My parents' story is one of continuous and endless sacrifice. I grew up in a family where resilience and adaptability were essential. My father, an agricultural engineer in Lebanon, lost his job during a difficult period, leaving him without a clear career path for several years. Despite his qualifications, he found himself working odd jobs, none of which aligned with his education or professional goals. After years of struggle, he finally secured a well-paying position, but it required him to move to Saudi Arabia, separating him from us.

For the first year, we remained in Lebanon, where my mother was a teacher, while he worked to stabilize his new life abroad. When the time was right, my parents decided to reunite the family, and we joined him in Saudi Arabia. It was a significant transition. My brother and I enrolled in one of the top schools in the country, and my mother got a job teaching at that same school. On the surface, everything seemed perfect. The school provided the best education available, and we were all together again. But there was a deeper struggle.

Saudi Arabia's cultural norms clashed deeply with my sense of identity and freedom. Women were not allowed to drive back then, and once I reached a certain age, I was forced to wear the traditional black abaya—a long, shapeless dress meant to cover any outline of the feminine body—and I had to cover my head as well. The idea of these restrictions being imposed on women was deeply frustrating to me, and I felt suffocated.

Adding to this was the oppressive heat and the dry desert climate, which only deepened my sense of isolation. I found it difficult to make friends, the environment left me feeling disconnected from everything familiar.

What troubled me most though, was the extreme way religion was practiced. Instead of feeling welcomed or guided by faith, I felt alienated by the rigidity and uncompromising rules. This pushed me to question everything around me, and I became increasingly rebellious, constantly arguing with my parents over these cultural and religious expectations that I simply couldn't accept.

Every weekend was a battle of emotions. I often found myself crying, struggling to reconcile my personal beliefs with what the society had forced upon me, as a woman.

The restrictions on women, the intense religious practices, and the isolation from a more open-minded environment weighed heavily on me. I knew that this life was not the one I wanted, and it shaped my determination to eventually break free from those constraints.

I simply did not fit in, and my parents, sensing my continuous distress, made the difficult decision to live apart once again. My mother, my brother, and I returned to Lebanon while my father remained abroad, working tirelessly for our future and our family. For thirteen long years, they navigated the complexities of separation with a quiet dignity, their love for their children serving as an unwavering compass.

Just two days before my husband's tragedy, my mother had submitted her retirement papers preparing to join my father again. My younger brother graduated, and the time was finally right for them to be together. But life added a cruel twist and threw another obstacle in their path, pulling them apart yet again. When my husband died, my father told my mother, "Our daughter needs you more than I do now." They once again sacrificed their togetherness for me. My mom withdrew her retirement papers and stayed to support me and my two boys.

My father eventually retired and returned to Lebanon, but only because he was very ill. My mother spent the last seven years of his life caring for him as his health deteriorated. Her love and dedication shone through until his last breath.

I was surrounded by quiet strength and unspoken sacrifices, things that went unnoticed until I found myself in the depths of my own grief. Their love was a lifeline, a reminder that even in the deepest despair, there are hearts that shine with a light that can never be extinguished.

Witnessing my friend's kindness and my parents' endless sacrifices made me stop and reflect on the beliefs we build around the people in our lives. It made me reconsider how we should look at others. In our greatest moments of need, this is when true humanity shines.

THE JOURNEY TO HEALING

In those early days of grief, still numb from shock, I was already beginning to see a positive shift in how I viewed the world. I needed to allow my spirit the space to feel everything—the pain, the loss, but also the love and kindness that surrounded me.

In the midst of this dark journey, I questioned everything.

This wasn't just about surviving the loss life had thrown at me; it was about finding a way to thrive, to build a new life for my children and for myself—a life where joy and fulfillment were not just memories but tangible realities.

One afternoon, my uncle sat across from me, sipping his coffee and offering words that were meant to comfort, but they struck me in a way I was not prepared for.

"Your life revolves around your children," he said, "that's where you'll find your joy."

I knew he meant well, but his words felt like a quiet dismissal of my very existence. Suddenly, I was not just grieving my husband—I felt like I was grieving myself, too. His attempt to soothe my pain instead made me feel small, sidelined, invisible. It was as if the only part of me that mattered was my motherhood, as if my life, my needs, my own desires had all vanished the moment I became a widow.

I love my children deeply, and parenting has always been the hardest job I have ever had, even more so now that I am doing it alone. But it was not my choice to walk this path—it was forced upon me when my husband died. Yes, I want to be the best mother I can be, to give my children safety, security, and a good future, but what about me?

Those words tumbled out before I could even stop them: "What about me?"

I needed to find my own strength, my own purpose. How could I be there for my children if I couldn't even hold onto my own identity?

His response—"Your strength comes from them."—only deepened the ache in my chest. I was not asking for a lecture about duty or a reminder of my responsibilities. I needed to hear that it was okay to still have desires, needs, dreams of my own. Instead, I felt erased, as if the only parts of me that mattered were those connected to being a wife before, and now a mother.

Was it selfish to still want something for myself? Was it wrong to think about my own needs, or was I only allowed to do so when it served my children?

In that moment, I wrestled with the cultural expectations that had long shaped my life. I was not ready to give up on the idea that I could still have a life of my own, that I could still dream and grow, despite my grief.

But how could I reconcile that with the pressure to find all my joy, all my strength, in my role as a mother?

I was not ready to let go of myself—not yet.

This was the moment where the disconnect between myself and the culture I had always known began to take root. I had always believed in the values and traditions I grew up with, but now I found myself questioning them.

Were they meant to guide me, or confine me?

The guilt was overwhelming, as if thinking about myself was a betrayal of my past, of my late husband, of my kids, of family and my culture.

It was a battle to overcome that guilt and to acknowledge that I, too, deserved to live and be happy.

As I wrestled with these feelings, a line was drawn in my mind: The life I had known, the person I had been, all was now behind that line.

Ahead of me was a new beginning. I was not the same person, not even the person I was a few months ago.

I refused to be defined by my grief.

There had to be more for me, more to my story, more than just sorrow.

The realization hit me. This was my moment. The rest of my life would start here.

I would thrive, not just for my children, but for myself too. Because if I did not have my own strength, how could I possibly give any to them?

I needed to retrieve my sense of self. Who am I? It was time to find out.

It was time for me to reclaim my identity, to learn how to prioritize myself without the crushing weight of guilt. I had to set boundaries—not just with my family, but with the unspoken expectations of society. I needed space to carve out moments of self-care, something I had been neglecting for far too long.

But grief has its own timeline. I started small. I bought a treadmill and committed to working out at least twice a day. It was not just about physical health—it was about giving myself permission to invest in me. Each run felt like I was slowly breaking free from the invisible chains of duty, guilt, and expectation. And yet, that was only part of the story.

I have always been social by nature, but as a widow, culture dictated that I should remain confined to my home unless absolutely necessary. Dancing, laughing with friends, or even showing a smile was not socially accepted for a widow. The role I was expected to play—constantly somber, always the embodiment of sadness—was suffocating. I made a decision: I was not going to live like that. I refused to be a shadow of myself.

I started going out again, but this time, I was careful about who I surrounded myself with. I needed people who understood my journey, friends who were my cheerleaders, not those who would judge me for trying to find moments of joy. It was not easy. Every time I smiled, there was a nagging thought telling me I should not. However, I owed it to myself to feel alive again.

I also sought emotional and mental support. I started seeing a psychiatrist to help me untangle the complex emotions I was dealing with, and I took my eldest child with me. I wanted him to have the tools to navigate his own healing, too. I connected with others who had gone through similar losses. Sharing our stories made me feel less alone and helped me realize that my pain did not have to define me forever.

Along this path, a shift took place—I stopped living in the past. I stopped waiting for life to return to how it used to be and started envisioning the future. It was not just about being a mother anymore. I started setting personal goals that were solely mine.

I planned a trip to Sri Lanka with my cousin—10 days to breathe, to rediscover the world, and to reconnect with myself outside of my grief and responsibilities. That trip was more than a getaway; it was a step toward building a new narrative.

The trip to Sri Lanka came about unexpectedly. My cousin Malak, who is also my best friend, knew—as only someone who truly knows you can—that I needed a break, a place where no one had expectations of me, where I could be whoever I wanted, or even just be quiet, without having to explain anything. Malak and I had been talking for weeks about how much I needed a break. She could see it in me, how my shoulders were weighed down. She said, "Let's go somewhere new. Just you and me." At first, I brushed it off. I had the kids to think about, the house, a thousand small things that kept me tied down.

Eventually, it was the idea of having a whole week where no one needed anything from me that made me say yes.

I told myself it would be fine; my mom would be with the kids, and there was no one else I'd trust more. Part of me felt guilty and selfish leaving my kids. However, I needed this time for myself, and having Malak beside me was such a gift. She is a beautiful soul—warm, funny, and one of those people who make life feel simpler and brighter. She understood that I just needed to let go for a while.

But still, when I hugged my children goodbye, there was a pang of guilt.

Knowing they were with my mom made it easier. She has such a gentle, loving way with them, and I knew she would care for them with all the love I would. Even as I boarded the plane, a part of me worried if it was wrong to leave, even just for a week. But Malak reminded me that this was a chance for me to breathe, to find a part of myself I had lost along the way.

On our first day, we visited an elephant orphanage. There, we saw an old, blind elephant that had been rescued. Watching her made me pause; she had such a peaceful presence, like she had found her own way of moving through the world. The scene was so simple, so natural, and it touched me deeply—this old elephant just being, without needing anyone's approval, her own kind of freedom. It was a reminder of the purity and beauty that still exists if you take the time to look for it.

Sri Lanka felt like a breath of fresh air. It felt like freedom in a way I hadn't felt in a long time, as if it was another world. The lush green landscape, the quiet way people moved through their day, unbothered by the rush of things, left me feeling grounded.

One morning, we left the door to our balcony open, and when we came back, monkeys had raided our room, leaving us with nothing to eat. It was the first time I could laugh about something like that, just enjoying the moment.

Being by the ocean was something new to me. I live by the Mediterranean, therefore I had never experienced waves like the ocean waves—powerful, relentless. Standing there, letting the water wash over me, it felt like it was cleansing something deep inside. Each wave felt like it was carrying away some of the weight I'd been holding, washing away my sorrow and bringing me hope. For those days, I felt a spark of my old self returning, like I was recovering a part of myself that had been lost.

I actively challenged the belief that my identity was limited to being a wife and a mother. I began rewriting my story to allow room for *me*, the individual. I allowed myself to dream again, to have desires, and to explore a life beyond what was expected of me.

I started by setting boundaries and carving out "me" time, moments that belonged just to me. I gave myself permission to breathe, to reflect, and to nurture the parts of myself that had been quieted since Tarek's passing. I allowed myself to slowly reconnect with friends, to go out and be social, to laugh freely, and, on some nights, even to dance, allowing life back into my heart. I indulged in small adventures, from solo outings to trying new things without worrying about judgment. I rediscovered the beauty of life's simple pleasures and gave myself permission to love life again—beyond roles or expectations. In these moments, I felt alive and whole, not just as a mother or a wife but as me.

And as I ventured further into this new chapter, I learned to embrace imperfections and uncertainty. I realized there was no perfect roadmap to follow. It was okay to take things one step at a time, to stumble and to adjust. This journey wasn't about getting it right—it was about moving forward, no matter how uncertain the path might seem.

Every step, every decision, was a reclaiming of myself.

However, those times were also a heartbreaking roller coaster of emotions, as I searched for my identity and tried to navigate the void left behind.

THE CLOSET

When I was not busy with work, my kids or friends, time moved so painfully slowly, and the emptiness inside me felt immense—so big, it was almost impossible to put into words.

I missed Tarek with an ache that cut to my core.

I remember standing in front of his closet, the place where I could still find traces of him.

I waited for those rare moments when I was alone in the house, craving the solitude that allowed me to lose myself in his scent.

I would slip into the closet, wrap myself in his clothes, and breathe him in. That small, dark space became my refuge, a warm blanket around my shattered heart.

I missed being loved. I missed being touched, hugged close.

Despite the incredible support and love from the friends and family around me, there was a specific kind of love that was missing—the kind that had filled every part of me, body and soul.

That love, his love, was gone, leaving behind a hollow ache.

I turned to the only way I knew to bring him back: by triggering my senses.

His clothes still carried the faint scent of him, a scent I refused to wash away. It was all I had left.

In that closet, I would cry, letting wave after wave of grief wash over me. I cried so many days, so many times, feeling the cruelty of life pressing down on me.

Sometimes, I could almost hear him.

The sound of the front door opening, his footsteps in the hall, the ring of my phone with his number flashing on the screen.

In my dreams, he would come back to me, and I would ask him, "Where were you? I'm glad you're back." But it was just a dream, a dream I woke up from every time to the stark reality that he was not coming back.

My faith was wrecked.

"It is God's will," my mom would say, trying to comfort me.

But I was furious, rebellious against that phrase. How could a good God allow such suffering?

It felt like evil had taken over my life. I hadn't chosen this. None of us had.

But by now, I understood that while the tragedy was beyond my control, my reaction to it was within my power. Taking back ownership of my life and my children's lives was up to me.

I continued questioning all the norms that didn't make sense to me.

Why must a widow wear black indefinitely, as if the longer she remains wrapped in darkness proves her loyalty to the one she lost?

Why should a widow not be seen laughing, enjoying life, or daring to dance at a party?

These expectations felt like iron chains, imprisoning me in my grief.

They added another layer of suffering to an already unbearable loss.

Life was already so unfair—why do we, people, allow these norms and traditions to make it even worse?

I started to break free from these chains. I challenged the rules that did not serve me, rules that seemed to exist only to make me feel more confined, more suffocated.

I was on the path to reclaiming my life on my own terms, even if it meant stepping into the light when the world expected me to stay in the shadows, time began to pass.

THE LIGHT AHEAD

A couple of years went by, with plenty of ups and downs, moments of strength followed by waves of doubt. I struggled within myself, constantly wrestling with the norms that dictated how a widow should behave. It felt like an endless fight between what was expected of me and what I truly wanted for myself.

Then, unexpectedly, someone showed up in my life—a friend of my deceased husband. He had been living in the United States for years, studying and building a life for himself, a life he could not have had if he had stayed in Lebanon. After over a decade in the US, he returned to visit his family and reconnect with old friends. That is when he learned that his friend, Tarek, had passed away and that he had left behind a wife and two boys. I never knew this person existed and I did not even meet him during that first visit, but he reached out to me on social media soon after.

When he introduced himself, asking about me and the boys, something felt different. For the first time in a long time, I felt like someone was asking about *me*—not just my role as a mother or a widow, but about how *I* was doing. He wanted to know what it was like for *me* now, navigating life after Tarek's death. And to be honest, he had a way of making me feel good about myself, something I hadn't felt in a long time. Our conversations were not regular, but we checked in with each other occasionally, and every time, it felt like a small, unexpected warmth.

Then, one day, about five months into our Facebook exchanges, we unexpectedly crossed paths at a beach resort during his second visit to Lebanon. For those who do not know, Lebanon is a very small country, and we were in a small city called Tripoli, where everyone knows everyone. So, it was not unusual to accidentally cross paths. I still remember that moment vividly. I was walking toward the beach with my two boys, holding their hands, and he was leaving the beach with his younger sister. Our eyes met, and we stopped, exchanged smiles, and talked. He was even more handsome than in his profile picture, I thought.

But it was not just a simple conversation, something shifted.

Right then, something felt different.

A part of me that had been dormant for so long was suddenly revived, as if a spark had been reignited deep inside me.

As I stood there, looking into his beautiful blue eyes, it was as if I could see a horizon stretching out before me—a new beginning, a promise of something I had never dared to imagine. Something inside me stirred. Feelings I had not allowed myself to feel. A strange mix of emotions swirling inside me. There was an undeniable sense of excitement, like a spark of light breaking through the darkness. Along with it came a hint of fear, the kind that makes your heart skip a beat because you are stepping into the unknown.

Shortly after, my phone rang. It was him. He asked when we could see each other again. My mind started racing. Could this be a new chapter? Just when I thought the curtain had fallen on my love life, that the final act had been played, the Universe surprised me with an encore. A new stage was set, a new story waiting to be written, a chance to experience love in a way I had never imagined. Could my husband's friend, this man who had known Tarek so well, be in my future?

I felt a storm of emotions swirling inside me—guilt, happiness, confusion. I knew they had been close, sitting on the same bench at school for an entire year in high school, going to the Boy Scouts together. I even looked back at old photos and saw them side by side, smiling and laughing. And now, here I was, contemplating a connection with someone who had shared so much history with Tarek. The guilt was immediate and overwhelming. Was it wrong for me to even consider this?

But amid that guilt, there was also a flicker of happiness. For the first time, I felt alive again in a way I had not since Tarek's passing. A part of me was daring to ask: Can I love again? Can I be loved again? Could I open my heart to this man, despite the history we shared, despite the complexity of it all?

The emotions inside me once again clashed, but this time at a deeper level—guilt for moving forward, happiness at the possibility of something new, and uncertainty about the future.

But at that moment, like so many before, I realized that even though the world might see me as a widow destined to stay in the shadows, I had the right to step into the light. I had the right to feel, to love, and to be loved again.

I could not deny that I felt something, an intuition telling me that this might be more than just a passing encounter. It was thrilling, yet terrifying. Could I really open my heart again, and to my late husband's friend? Someone who had once been a part of Tarek's life, and now was unexpectedly stepping into mine? Could this be the beginning of something new? I did not have the answers, but the questions lingered, heavy and uncertain.

I knew there were no guarantees ahead, but one thing was certain—I was willing to challenge the expectations, to listen to my own intuition, and to find a path that felt true to me. A part of me was ready to take the risk and *decide* what was right for me, even if it meant stepping beyond the bounds of what I'd always known.

Now, I want to take a moment to shine a light on the setbacks and struggles that so many of us endure—the emotional strain of a relationship breaking apart, or the countless waves of challenges that knock us off our feet hits hard, and it does not play fair. What I have learned, and what I want to share, is that every single one of us has strength inside—a resilience—that we can build and nurture, even when it feels like the world has gone dark.

When I lost Tarek, my world collapsed. Grief consumed me, and there were days when it felt like I was buried under the weight of it all. But there was a voice within me, a small yet persistent voice, that reminded me that I was not done yet.

And so, I began to rebuild. As I began to rebuild, my life started to shift in small but profound ways. I turned my focus inward, reclaiming the parts of myself that I had neglected. I started paying attention to my health—not just physically, but emotionally. I became more active, prioritizing movements that felt good and brought me energy. Time with my kids transformed into something sacred. We created happy moments together, filled with laughter, silliness, and the kind of joy that feels like sunlight breaking through clouds. Weekends found me at my cousins' homes more often, where I rediscovered a sense of peace I had not felt in years. There, I could simply *be*. No masks, no pretense—just myself. Slowly, the comfort I found with them gave me the courage to shed those masks everywhere else. I stopped accepting the status quo, those rules and expectations I had once nodded along to without question. I started saying no. Each "no" felt like a step toward freedom, a defiance of the invisible boundaries that had held me back for so long. It was not just about rejecting what did not serve me—it was about finding my voice, and using it. I realized that rebuilding was not about returning to who I was before; it was about becoming someone stronger, someone who could claim her space in the world unapologetically.

It was not easy, There were moments of doubt, of uncertainty, of questioning whether we were truly meant to be. But through it all, we persevered, our commitment to each other deepened.

I had to find that circle of influence within myself, that place where I could plant the seeds of resilience.

I focused on what I could control—my actions, my mindset—and I learned to accept what I could not.

Building resilience is not just about surviving; it's about finding a way to thrive, even when everything around you feels like it is falling apart.

Was this the light at the end of the tunnel I had been searching for?

Or was it another challenge, one that would test my ability to trust my instincts, to see the good in others, and to decide what was right for me, even if it defied the norms I had grown up with?

I knew there were no guarantees, but one thing was certain—I was willing to challenge the expectations, to listen to my own intuition, and to follow the path that felt true to me.

The journey ahead was uncertain, and it wouldn't be without its challenges. But for the first time in a long while, I felt like I was moving toward something, rather than away from the past. Could this be the beginning of a new chapter? Could this handsome man, with his warm smile and kind eyes, be the light I had been waiting to find?

Pakinam (Paki) Fawal is a writer, project manager, and advocate for resilience and cultural transformation. Originally from Lebanon, she holds a bachelor's degree in computer science and spent years teaching and shaping young minds before transitioning to project management.

Now a Project Manager at Dexcom, Pakinam empowers people to take control of their health—a mission deeply personal to her, as her youngest daughter lives with type 1 diabetes.

As a devoted wife and loving mom to three, Pakinam values family, growth, and community. She is currently writing a memoir exploring cultural expectations, personal freedom, and resilience to inspire others to embrace their unique paths.

Repairing the Sorrows of My Past

BY KRISTINA GREEN

"I'm having a baby by someone else."

He said the words calmly with a drink in his left hand and our good friend, Andre, to his right. You would imagine these words to spark outrage and a whirlwind of emotions. But no. Surprisingly, his words brought relief and calm to the torrential storms of my mind that tormented me each time my calls were unanswered or each night he did not come home. The hurt and sadness were subsiding and releasing their grasp on my already broken heart. After years spent ignoring the signs, I was surprisingly comforted by the truth. It was almost as if I had to be told directly that my marriage was a lie before I would allow myself to believe it.

For twenty-plus years and almost five years of marriage, he was all I knew. But our days were always numbered. Painfully, I endured the infidelity of my first love more times than I can recall. My heart was in its infancy and attached to a man who lacked the emotional maturity to love me in the ways I needed and deserved.

When I close my eyes, I can still remember that moment. I was seated on the living room chair. My body was hot with anticipation of what I was going to hear. I closed my eyes for long pauses as I tried to avoid his smug face as he took sips of his liquid courage, as if to prolong the news and keep me in suspense.

And then it came. The words flowed from his intoxicated lips, "I am having a baby by someone else", and he was finally speaking in a frequency I understood, the truth.

Our friend was there for moral support and truthfully to keep us from turning a heartbreaking situation into a devastating one. I do not know what would have become of us had he not been there, and I am so grateful that he was.

Andre encouraged him to "come clean and tell her everything". My ex would take a few more sips before the rest of the truth—at least what he was willing to say—came out.

For what felt like an hour, in a house we thankfully did not own together, I listened to him tell me about his affairs. None of which surprised me—well, maybe one, but that is a story for another day and a bottle of bourbon. After enduring multiple recounts of moments where he was unreachable and countless nights I spent alone in our bed crying and feeling foolish for ever trusting my heart to him. I began disassociating from the man I once called "the love of my life".

I had been doing all I could to 'keep up appearances' of a family that never existed. I desperately wanted to believe that having the 'traditional family', with the kids and the husband, would somehow make all of my insecurities disappear. That somehow, if I could create the perfect life—one that was the opposite of everything I had known as my reality—perhaps I would learn to love myself. I wanted to feel like I belonged to something greater than myself. A family was that for me and apparently, I was willing to sacrifice and lower my expectations to get it.

The next few days after hearing the devastating news were a blur. I could not bring myself to make such an impossible decision, especially not in the heat of the moment. So, I allowed myself time to tune into my own thoughts and come to a decision. Was I to trust that we could make this work? Or was that just another fairytale?

Three nights later, we were entangled in an emotional discussion. Tears were flowing and promises were being made that "We can make this work." I wanted to believe that we could put the lid back on to Pandora's box and find a way forward. In a frantic state of trying to save my marriage—to save the facade I was portraying to the world about my marriage—I said, "You can't be there for her birth."

Words I regret to this day because they were spoken in a selfish and hurtful rage. At the time my world was unraveling. But these would be the words that would unlock the 'me' I had tucked away long before. Those hurtful words would deliver me from the lies I kept telling myself to keep me in a trance. They were the poison I had methodically dispensed in an effort to *'protect'* my heart.

They shook my senseless mind free from the love spell I had voluntarily stepped into decades before and gave me back my self-worth. That little girl did not deserve the reality of those words to come to pass and I knew it, even in the moment when my heart felt like it could not have broken anymore. I was shedding a skin that I had outgrown long before because I was morphing into who I had always been.

As I said those words, I knew that I did not want this to be my life any longer. I knew I was settling for less than I deserved.

Little did I know that his daughter, born from his affair, would become one of the greatest gifts. Not only because she had awoken me from autopilot mode of a failing marriage, but because she reminded me of the person I had buried deep inside long ago.

It took me until 34 years old, when I was faced with the hardest decision of my life, to finally stop maintaining the lies of the status quo and to instead, accept the uncomfortable truths I had buried and known all along. I needed to separate from a relationship that no longer served me.

I had reached the end of my tolerance. This was not to be my life any longer. A new chapter was to begin, and it started with me walking away from the lies and walking toward the unknown truths that awaited me.

It was time for a divorce.

While I will tell you briefly that my husband was a habitual cheater, my purpose in doing so is not for sympathy or even in solidarity with others who have experienced the painful events of having an unfaithful spouse. He caused pain in my life that felt insurmountable. But the truth is that my connection with his daughter, born from an affair, was far from a source of pain and sorrow for me. Quite the opposite. While her existence catapulted me into divorce, that little girl became my heart song and the catalyst for me to reconnect with my inner child.

I did not know it at the time, but she set me on a healing journey to repair the sorrows of my past. A journey to reconcile the roots of my insecurities that allowed me to settle for less than I deserved for years. Although my journey began with tears it has blossomed into one of triumph through self-love and authenticity.

Before the tears formed the stream to my future, there were many hard days.

I remember the first time I saw his daughter. It was a typical Southern California day, ripe with sunshine, and the hustle of busy households moving in and out of the Gelson's parking lot. As usual, I parked and was awaiting the arrival of my ex-husband to do our weekly parent exchange. Those days were so hard, watching my boys shuffle between homes toting carry-on bags of clothing and unspoken words of disappointment. Divorce is not easy, but it is especially hard on the kids. I saw it on their faces each day as their father and I were trying to find a 'new normal' for such an unnatural reality.

Most days I felt on the brink of tears, contemplating how I was going to put on my best smile and pretend that the decades of love that was now lost were of no consequence. Pretending that I was fine. All was fine and I did not need anyone, let alone him, in my life.

No matter my preparation, the feeling of betrayal took a long time to forgive because the wounds were still tender, even after a year of separation.

How is this my life? I thought to myself.

I had lived so little to know so much pain at just 35 years old.

How was I to prevent my boys from developing resentment towards me for drastically altering their lives?

I knew I had made the right decision but it has never felt good to have to make it. I was watching the reality of those decisions play out right in front of my eyes, but it was not until that day in the parking lot that I understood just how important that decision was for my future and the future of my children.

He pulled up alongside my parked car and my boys began to spill out, carrying bags of clothes and local fast food. I walked around the back of my car to open the trunk and I heard my oldest son, Michael, say "Bye, Lily!" I was stunned and became frozen in the moment. I thought to myself, *'Oh my goodness! She's with them?'* I had never laid eyes on his little girl before. I was almost terrified to do so.

As my boys piled all of their stuff into my trunk, I followed my curiosity to the rear passenger window of my ex-husband's car and there she was—his beautiful little girl, no more than a year old now. I was not prepared for what would come next. I had internalized a nightmare response that I would cry out of control at the sight of her precious face, making the nightmare into a reality. And even worse, I would do all of it in front of my ex—a man I had loved for over two decades and who had broken my heart in unimaginable ways. I had decided long before then that he would not witness my pain nor would he be part of my joy ever again. So, I kept my overwhelming excitement and endearment to myself.

But when I saw her face, the warmest feeling of love and joy flowed through me. A feeling I had only experienced with my own children, but was now fully present and experiencing in the Gelson's parking lot as I stared at her angelic face. This little girl saved me in ways she would never understand.

She turned her head quickly acknowledging my presence. Searching for familiarity, she gazed at me with her bright eyes, studying my features. I too could not take my eyes off of her. Her messy ponytail was wrangled by the car seat. Her mouth paused, slightly open as if I caught her mid-sentence calling for her brothers. Completely captivated by her soft spirit, I smiled and waved, to which she gave me a perplexed smile. She didn't know me, but in that moment I felt the fears and the pains of the life I had lost with my ex-husband replaced with joy and purpose for a life that awaited us both.

Setting my eyes upon Lily launched me into the most important journey of my lifetime. Her birth had triggered the end of a marriage that had run its course and ignited a spark that would guide me to fulfill a life of authenticity. I knew at that moment, with a car window between us and as our eyes met for the first time, that we were both living our purpose. She was to be the redirection I needed to claim my future, and I was to be the distant 'mother' figure who would carry her in my heart.

But I hear you asking, "How did you find your way to love a little girl that was the product of your husband's betrayal?"

The journey of forgiving my ex is separate from learning to love myself and extending that love to a little girl who guided me there. Through her beautiful existence, I reconnected with the deepest part of myself that I had turned away from many years before to appease a relationship that was never rightly suited for me. Yes, his actions ended our marriage, but that was inconsequential to all that I gained through my rebirth.

His daughter has been and will always be a gift to me. Not only because she saved me from a failing marriage, but because she reminded me of the person I had buried deep inside long ago.

But I understand how this still is not quite fathomable for most to believe. So, let me tell you how the world not only shaped me into who I had always been, but whom I had tucked away to claim a life I thought I wanted.

Raised as an only child between my mother and father, but the second oldest of five girls by my father, I had a confused sense of what family was. I was estranged from my half-sisters and when I was just 6-years-old, my parents moved me from Seattle to Los Angeles. To be honest, I don't recall interacting with them in my early childhood. I am not certain I even knew I had sisters at 6-years-old. What I understood about family played itself out in the rocky relationship between my parents, which ultimately led to their separation when I was a teenager.

All I learned about relationships was through my environment, which included television. As a kid and young adult, television provided structure and problem-solving to scenarios I had not even experienced yet, especially for those of us who were 'latch-key' children navigating the world to and from school in grade school on our own. Today, we would never dream of allowing our children this exposure to the world, but it was a different time then.

I grew up watching after-school shows and cooking my own meals because my parents worked full-time and often did not arrive until early evening.

I lived through fictional characters and used to dream of long-lasting relationships of love and devotion that I saw these characters had on those shows. Couples like the Huxtables were the epitome of what I was aiming for. Clair Huxtable was who I imagined when I pictured mothering my own hypothetical children. I even remember practicing her long stare in the mirror with my cabbage patch babies. Yes, it takes a lot of practice to be this sassy.

In grade school, we were tasked with an assignment to create a book of our future, in which we were to draw various scenes of how we pictured that future. One page in my book was a hospital nursery with two bassinets. One for a boy and the other for a girl. Their names were clearly displayed above as Michael and Shelby. Yes, I loved the movie "Steel Magnolias" even as a young girl in grade school. And fun fact, my oldest son's name is Michael.

I was obsessed with having a family and never considered a future career. It just didn't enter my thoughts. Yes, I would dream of being a singer, an actress, and a model but I never considered dreams to be reality. They simply filled the space and sufficed the question from adults, *"What do you want to be when you grow up?"* Honestly, I had no idea what I wanted to do or who I wanted to be, but I always knew I wanted a family.

As a young adult, I would binge-watch the Father of the Bride movies, daydreaming about my 'wedding at home" which was certainly a dream because I have lived in an apartment most of my life. I would watch the men acquiesce with their wives and girlfriends on TV although that was never the case in my home.

My father was a strong-willed partner in constant pursuit of his dream of 'making it big in entertainment' and would rather die than have anyone tell him what to do. My mother, having raised herself from her teens, was equally as strong, and raised me pretty much on her own because my dad was always chasing his dreams and working long hours. The semblance of 'family' I had was skewed, but I never thought it was wrong or bad. I just never gave it much thought because television offered an alternative perspective that I wanted more.

It was then that I started building an imaginary world where hurt did not exist and love was overflowing. It did not mimic my reality and gave me an escape and a chance to experience something different. After all, the characters on television seemed to solve all of their issues within an episode, so hurt did not last and perhaps did not even exist in this fictional place. I wanted my life to be just like theirs. My 'knight in shining armor' would be my hero and deliver me from a life of ordinary and make all of my dreams a reality.

Through the embodiment of these false realities that I had either witnessed on television or made up in my head, I was unknowingly creating the hammer that was to one day break my own heart. I had set standards on which to measure my happiness all based on relationships and family structures that were fabricated and imaginary. No one was capable of living up to the flawless life I had dreamt of, yet it did not stop me from projecting that expectation onto my relationships.

Age has taught me that real life is only partially told through the stories of sitcoms and screenplays. Even nowadays, the stories of struggles and hardships on the 'big screen' always have a layer that remains untouched. There is a corner where light cannot reach and a space where life is felt and experienced that may never be told. They are the seemingly insignificant moments, simple grains of sand, that collectively make up the shores of our lives. They are ever-changing and reshaping with each wave that life brings us. We are actively living our testimony through the case studies we call life.

Countless times I ignored the truth and replaced it with a lie–a fantasy I had cooked up in my head because the reality was not living up to my expectations. I made excuses for painful truths as an act of self-preservation. For decades I allowed myself to exist in this imaginary world where truth was non-existent and pain could not penetrate. I wanted to believe my relationship was solid and rooted in love and devotion. Lying to myself I let these fantasies take over my reality because it was easier to believe than the truth.

But now, I wonder if I could have spared myself the painful experiences orchestrated by my disbelief in reality by allowing myself to see with my eyes rather than my imagination. Could I have saved my heart from breaking had I 'grown up' a bit sooner?

We were immature when we began blending our lives, and now, over 25 years later, I know that I cannot live in regret but rather sit with my humility and gratitude for the life experiences that have shaped me. Yes, I broke my own heart for decades, and as I reflect on this fact, I am grateful for the experience because I was finally able to break free from the imaginary land where relationships were flawless. I have grown past enforcing my expectations on others and have chosen to focus on doing the self-reflective deep work that welcomes my most authentic self.

It is heartbreaking to consider that I was not only an active participant in my pain, but that I was actually the creator. Sadly, it is true. Living outside of reality only leads to disappointment because even our definition of love, endearment, and relationships evolves as we move through our experiences.

Now, this is not to say that I hold 100% of the blame for the ending of my marriage but more so to acknowledge my part in how it unfolded.

We can prevent our suffering simply by living in reality and pursuing our desires rather than creating a series of unrealistic expectations of others to live up to.

Manifesting a desired reality is not only possible, I've lived it. I created a direct line to me for exactly what I did not want by living in this false reality. I was terrified to speak my desires into existence so I spoke words from others and I got exactly what I asked for, but it turned out to be the opposite of what I wanted.

I got a long-standing relationship with my 'ideal mate' that looked good on paper but felt empty and one-sided. You never consider the nights you may spend crying over the unrequited love of your life, or how painful the evolution of a young love shifts as you both grow.

I got to build a family with beautiful children but at what cost? My children had to endure my immaturity and grew to understand the pain of what divorce does to children.

My experiences have taught me that extending grace and flexibility for others to be exactly who they are is a loving act towards you both. Stop auditioning for characters in your life and start holding space for the authenticity of others.

This revelation has taken me decades to absorb. I have wasted years molding myself to fit the ideals I shaped into beliefs in childhood rather than diving more deeply into my truth. I set aside my beliefs to align with those of my partner and became surprised when I had no idea who I was or what I liked when my marriage failed. I sculpted my entire life around this idea of a family and my world crumbled when I was faced with the life-altering decision to take a bulldozer to all I had spent decades building.

Why does any of this matter?

Why have I chosen to tell you this story?

It was my first night alone in my new apartment, for my new life, and a new awakening. My boys were off with their father and I was all alone. I had never been alone. There was always someone in my presence to talk to, to do something with, but I was all by myself now. I turned off the television and listened to the quiet noise that was disrupting my thoughts. I gazed out my window at the streetlight peering through. The sound of cars driving by and revving their engines was no match to the voice in my head that felt like it was screaming, "We did it!"

"Did what, exactly?" I thought. I had never felt more alone. My boys were my company in this new space and without them, I did not know what to do with myself. I felt defeated and vulnerable because I had no person to attach myself to.

That was the problem, I had created a dependency on the need for distraction to prevent myself from facing the truth. My reality was held together by finely sewn seams that were easily pulled apart. The frayed ends of those seams were exposed and my truth was naked and visible. I was at a crossroads. I could either see this moment and all that followed as life happening to me and remain passive in how the future would unfold. Or I could meet the challenge that evolution demands and view this as an opportunity to grow in new and beautiful ways.

You are reading my story because I chose the latter. I chose to embrace the path I had avoided for decades because I believed something better awaited. Even if I had no idea of what it would be or when it would arrive.

So, I set out on a journey to experience all life had to offer.

I had withdrawn from building new friendships because I wrapped all of myself into my relationship. I thought I knew what I needed about friendships, but I was so wrong. I was missing out on the richness of relationships outside of intimacy that only comes through sharing the stories of our human experience. Growing up, the sitcom fairytale stories from a crafty storyteller shaped my worldview. Whether it was accurate or not was of no significance to me then. But now, I realize just how profound of an impact they had on how I chose to live my life.

I have chosen to share the stories of my human experience to be another voice that provides a glimpse into a life that you may see as a common thread. I tuned out the realities of my life desperately seeking to grasp life, love, and experience portrayed by made-up characters. But I am very much real and these stories are imperfect but they are very much mine.

Life is not handed to us on a silver tray and served with a side of honey. We live for the purpose of living and feeling the ebb and flow of life, but that is not meant to be a secret we keep to ourselves. We do ourselves and others a great disservice when we suffer in silence and withdraw our testimony from the world. As the orators of our history, we are inclined to bring voice to our experiences so that others can build upon our strength and grasp a life meant for them.

In all honesty, I did not want to tell this story because it reveals so much of the truth and forces me to relive moments I have tried so deeply to forget. So, the journey to place each word on this page was a battle I fought within. I had to create a safe space where boundaries were formed so that my story could flow as it was meant to. There are streams to this story that I have not yet told you, and perhaps they will one day find their voice or they may stay locked away. We endure and fight the battles we are prepared for and save those we are not for another day when we are braver than the current moment can hold.

I would not have this story to tell you or the many stories that followed it had it not been for the battles I waged within. I have not lived this life perfectly, but I have done so with integrity stained with flaws and misconstrued intentions. And I would not change any of it. I regret nothing because it has brought me exactly where I am today.

When I started my journey, I was heartbroken, and picking up the pieces wasn't easy. I was used to having a 'partner' in life and someone to share my wins with. All of that disappeared the day I chose to stop living in the passenger seat. It all changed when I was forced to scrape up what little was left of my heart from the pavement and forge ahead into the terrifying unknown.

Today, I look back, and I see strength that I once believed was weakness. I feel pride for the woman who was so bold to say 'no' to pennies knowing she was worth millions. That woman inspires me every day! She was the first of her kind in this story of Kristina. She formed the foundation for all versions that would follow her and I am steeped in gratitude for her always.

She made me a better mother, one who listens with intent and understanding and leans in with love rather than authority. She elevated our lives by diving into unknown careers we were born to do. She turned that once-afraid, doubtful, single mother into a first-time homeowner.

So, every day I have the privilege of awakening to sunlight shining through the window of a house that became a home, to a life of love and joy, all of which was possible because of the existence of a little girl who was destined to impact the world and she started with me.

Whether you choose to accept it or not, our lives are entangled with one another. Embracing our shared journey not only reveals your true purpose, but it inspires some of the best transformations you could ever know.

The hardest part of living is allowing yourself to do so. You may doubt whether it is even possible to live the life you dream, but it is. Each day I am blessed by the reality of my freedom that was once only a vision and a dream. Years ago, I stepped away from my corporate life and took a major leap of faith into the unknown. I started a business and built new friendships that have been crucial to my growth. My days are no longer full of things I 'have to' complete. Instead, I craft my days around the work I truly enjoy. I finally have the freedom of time I had only dreamt of years ago.

My successes are impossible without the experiences of who I once was and the journey I have taken to get here. Today, I am rich in loving relationships, I have a growing business, and each day I am accompanied by an ever-growing self-belief that all I have ever dreamt of is not only possible, it already exists. Where there once was doubt, is now replaced by countless receipts of action and experience.

Each stroke of the brush that has colored my life has created the painting that is my reality. Now, I step forward with intention and great appreciation for the woman who endured so much and grew despite setbacks. My story is far from over. It is actually just beginning.

We learn much from self-reflection and appreciation for our journey. Unveiling the rough edges of my story has been hard to share and I have had to grow along this journey. What better way to begin my next chapter than on the other side of vulnerability and authenticity?

Kristina Green is a Los Angeles based boy mom who ditched the corporate hustle amidst the pandemic with a crazy idea that something more awaited her. She was right. Since trading in the golden handcuffs for entrepreneurship in 2022, she has become the self-made woman that she never dreamed was possible but had always hoped to become. Carving out a new life for herself, her two boys, and her mother wasn't easy and yet it was worth every sacrifice. She's faced the darkest corners of her reality battling the shadows of unresolved poor self-image and self-doubt to emerge as a strong and courageous woman of great character. She's battled the pains of more than one heartbreak and lives to tell her stories so others might find their own strength. She now runs a consulting business advising professionals and corporations on how to manage and thrive with a multigenerational workforce. She is also a twice published author. Connect with Kristina on Instagram at kristinam.green, on Linkedin at kristina-m-green, or on her website cardigancareers.co.

Finding Ease

BY KELLY FEENEY

PART 1: A LITTLE GIRL IN FLIGHT

I want to start by talking about a little girl I know.

There's a little girl, her earliest memory is at 5 years old—her father throwing plates to the ground. One by one. Yelling at her mother, "Is that enough? Do you want to keep going?" She watches as he continues throwing plates at the ground, each plate shattering in pieces against the tile floor, until he has the last word. With each response from her mother, he throws another plate. "Stop it!" she yells. He slams another plate to the floor, irate and unable to control himself.

He does not remember how the argument started, how it ended, or anything else from that day.

Her childhood is marked by an absence of memories.

The girl remembers always feeling that what she witnessed was wrong, it was not normal. She knew it was not acceptable for adults to behave that way. She constantly wondered when it would end, when would her mom say enough, and remove her and her sister from this chaotic house.

It was always a house, never a home.

Her next memories are in a different house—the family moved regularly as her father changed jobs, or because he decided to go to law school across the country, or the owners of the property they were renting were moving back into the home. Each move meant a new school for her, and new neighbors who the little girl always knew heard her father's yelling and pretended everything was normal when she looked at them.

A total of six houses (and six new schools) across two states growing up.

Six times between kindergarten and high school graduation, she had to make new friends at schools where all the kids seemed to know each other since kindergarten. They had their friend circles established, years of memories, built up trust, and had their own inside jokes. It was hard enough to repeatedly make new friends as a child, and with the chaos at home, it added to her stress.

In the next house after the dish-throwing-house, she is now in 3rd grade. She has a few more memories at this age—playing with the kids next door when a tornado warning sounded and they hid in the basement and read books until it was over.

But a more detailed memory she carries is her mom waking her and her sister up in the middle of the night to pick her father up. He was at the police station with a DUI. When the family arrives to pick him up, he's yelling at the officers. *How embarrassing,* she thought, not only that he got a DUI, but that he's making a huge scene and yelling at the police officers who took him off the road in the name of safety. How embarrassing that others are not witness to the level of drinking he'd partake in inside their home.

The family moves three more times before she graduates high school.

She excelled in school and always played soccer as she changed neighborhoods, but she struggled to fit in as many schools had cliques and she was always the new kid. It took time, but she always managed to eventually make a core group of friends.

The vast majority of her core memories of her teenage years are filled with constant fighting at home and lots of yelling. *Lots of yelling.*

Her most vivid memory though, was finding her voice and standing up for her mom against her dad's daily abuses. The moments when she stood up for what was right.

"Stop talking to Mom that way!"

"Why don't you stop drinking and order food on your own?"

She'd say, yelling back to her father. Multiple times a day.

She'd repeat them until her voice was hoarse. Things no child should have to say, she was always self-aware of this. She remembers being cognizant from the beginning, as if she could zoom out to the future and know one day she'd have to move out, to move far away from the chaotic home she was forced to live in.

She also remembers the rancid smell of cigarettes. In the house. In the car. In her clothes.

One day, the kids at school made comments about her clothes smelling like cigarettes. She sat in class in silence, at a loss for words. The embarrassment stung. There was no part of the home that wasn't infested with the suffocating smell of cigarettes. She couldn't hide the smell that infiltrated its way into the deepest fibers of her clothes and there was no perfume that could cover it up.

Driving anywhere with a chain smoker felt like the worst punishment. Their car had an even more unpleasant smell than the house, a putrid, overwhelming scent, and he would barely even open the windows.

Once a year she was forced to endure the 20-minute car ride to her aunt's house for Thanksgiving, a trip she couldn't get out of and she couldn't convince her mom to drive two separate cars. On these rides, he'd urgently light a cigarette the moment her family said goodbye to her aunt's family. As soon as the car started, he'd like a cigarette. There was no care given to the two children in the car, even with her pleading, begging, and yelling at him to stop smoking.

"Your cigarettes are disgusting, stop forcing us to be in the car with this smell."

She would ask, insist, demand he not smoke in the house. Or at the very least, not smoke in the same car or room as them.

To cope, she stuck her head out the window like a dog, no matter how cold she was. She was set on breathing fresh air instead of the cigarette-smoke filled car, even if it meant she shivered the entire drive home. Her father did not pay attention to her begging him not to smoke in the house or car. Her mom, a nurse, also did not stand up to him with the health concerns of the family forced to constantly endure the second-hand smoke.

While her father was yelling at her mother, almost daily, she remembers using her voice to stand up for her mother. To stand up to what she always knew was wrong, to stand up to his abuse, which no other adult or family member was willing to.

"Do NOT talk to her that way, do NOT talk that way to anyone." She'd insist, as if she was the adult in the room.

She always had a strong conviction that it was not acceptable, that no father should treat their family this way, that it should never be anyone's normal.

She could not sit idly by in the house and *not* speak up. Her voice was too strong. She was very aware that her friends did not speak to their parents like this. However, this little girl knew what she was experiencing was not right. What was right, was to speak up against it. To never sweep it under the rug by avoiding it, by not addressing it like all of the other adults in her life did.

As the chaos continued in the house, life kept happening around her.

One day in 8th grade, she was playing soccer, one of the activities she absolutely loved. When she was on the field, this was one place she felt like she belonged, a place where she could focus on something outside of the frustration she felt. She had a strong kick so her coach would assign most free kicks to her. During this game, she felt an odd click in her knee. She told her mom, coach, and a few players. It did not hurt though. She kept playing. She had just scored a goal off of a corner kick—what a thrilling feeling! Next, the ref called a penalty and a free kick was awarded to her team. She was up to take it. As soon as she planted her left foot, winding up her right foot to strike the ball, she collapsed on the ground.

Her knee cap snapped to the back of her knee. She screamed in excruciating pain. A pain she had never felt—and to this day—has never felt before. Her knee was dislocated, and she quickly entered physical therapy.

During physical therapy, they sent her on a stationary bike. It was so painful, almost as painful as when her knee dislocated. She told the physical therapist and her mom she couldn't do the bike exercises. She told them that the pain she felt was not normal. They pushed her to continue, noting the rotation was good for her knee.

Later, a doctor would request a new x-ray that showed her knee cap was shattered. The x-ray looked like a cracked windshield. The entire patella was shattered into hundreds of pieces. She went into emergency surgery the next morning. The doctor removed 30% of her left patella and put 2 screws in to hold the remaining pieces together.

Why hadn't the adults listened to her when she expressed to them that the pain was excruciating and something else was wrong during weeks of physical therapy? Why hadn't her own mother, a nurse, listened to her when she insisted something was wrong and the pain was too much for her to bear?

She was using her voice, much like she had to at home, but no adults seemed to be listening.

Recovering from surgery was rough. She was only 14 years old and was used to playing sports. Now, she was trapped in her house, only able to go from her bed to a chair to the couch, and even that was painful. She had to stand up every few hours to get the blood flowing, but as soon as the blood rushed down her knee, the pain was excruciating. She could feel a burning, rushing sensation running down her knee.

Aside from losing her mobility, she lost a key part of how she coped with her chaotic home: her ability to leave the house. She couldn't even go run errands with her mom. She was stuck in the cigarette-smoke house full of constant, never-ending yelling.

One of many fights sparked at the dinner table during this time. She can't remember what sparked this fight, they all blend together with her father's perpetual anger and drinking.

Like any other day in her house, the fight started at the dinner table between her father and mother. Then, like clockwork, a fight started between her and her father. That's how it always went, a predictable pattern, another day in the life.

He was yelling at her; she was talking back to defend herself. But her mom and dad only understood it as talking back. They could not—they refused—to see the bigger picture, that she only spoke this way because no one would stand up to her father when he yelled at her mother. Even her own mother wouldn't speak up for herself or her children, so the responsibility fell to this little girl.

After she finished eating, she limped her way to the couch in the TV room, a nook connected to the dining room. She put her leg up on the couch, trying to get into a comfortable position for her knee. Her father continued the fight from the dinner table, a few steps away.

All of a sudden, he came and sat next to her, lugging the chair from the dining room, and placing it next to the couch. He lit a cigarette and smoked it right next to her, smoke billowing in her face.

She begged him to leave the room. Begged, pleaded, demanded, yelled. If a neighbor would have heard this, it would have sounded like the desperate cry of a kid who needed help.

Normally, she would just leave the room and go back to her room, close the door, and escape his behavior. This time, she physically could not move. She lost her only escape—her flight mode.

Her mom watched as this happened, not saying a word in her child's defense—not one word. She cried and begged her mom to please ask him to move away, to get the cigarette smoke out of her face. Her mom still did not say a word.

As the years went on, the yelling would increase. The fighting would increase.

Any chance she got to leave the house she would. If friends invited her over, she was there. If her mom needed to run an errand—any errand—she was waiting in the car by the time her mom grabbed her keys.

Quite literally any opportunity to leave the house, she took. She constantly lived in flight mode, something she wouldn't realize was a survival mechanism until later in life.

Flight Mode
A constant state of heightened stress, where this little girl quite literally took any opportunity, she could to leave her house (running errands, sports, going to friends' houses, etc...). A constant want, a need, to be away from her chaotic house.

She'd often tell her parents, "Get a divorce, do *not* stay together for the kids, no one wants this." She constantly wondered why her mother put up with someone talking to her the way her father spoke.

That wonder turned to frustration. *If you aren't leaving him out of respect for yourself, why not leave to set the right example to your children?*

This little girl always knew what she was witnessing, knew what she was living with was wrong. Somehow, she had no fear of speaking up to her father. She had no fear of using her voice. It was a responsibility she felt she had, to speak up to him on behalf of her mother. If her mother, or sister, never used their voices to express how wrong this all ways she knew she had to use hers.

Eventually, sometime in her teenage years, her mother would start to fight with her too. This was a turning point in their relationship. What started as a daughter speaking up on behalf of a mother that would not stand up for herself, or her children, turned into a mother's resentment towards her daughter.

The constant fighting in the house started to wear her mother down. Her father had convinced her mother that their daughter was the cause of the fights, a troubled, angry adult passing the blame onto his child. Now, when she would stand up for her mother, her mother would snap back at her daughter. "Stay out of it! You're making it worse."

That still did not stop her, she knew it wasn't her fault, and she knew she had a responsibility to herself to use her voice. But the betrayal stung.

How dare her mother put that blame on her daughter? Why couldn't her mother speak up for herself? Why couldn't her mother finally recognize her daughters were suffering? As a mother, how could she put her child in a position to feel the need to speak up for the entire family?

The fighting got worse when her father lost his job. A middle-aged man, a lawyer, lost his job sometime near the end of her high school years. Her parents wouldn't tell the children directly, but this little girl started to notice her father was home from work more than often.

She normally had the mornings in the house to herself—a time she savored where she could peacefully get ready for in the morning. They lived around the corner from her school and her parents always left for work early. She'd wake up to her radio alarm set to the local pop and hip-hop station 94.9, get ready at home, and then walk to school alone.

As she got ready for her day, she opened the window in the bathroom for some fresh air while she showered, got dressed, and put on the trendiest lip gloss and perfume to try her best to mask the smell of the cigarette smoke that permeated the walls (usually Love Spell, Sweet Pea, or Clinique Happy, this was the early 2000s after all). It was a rare moment where she was in her house alone, without yelling.

All of a sudden, her father was home in the morning. When she walked home after school, he was also there. It wasn't before long she figured out, he wasn't working. It was an unspoken but obvious observation.

Her peace in the morning was gone. She left the house as quickly as possible, avoiding speaking to him in the morning and after school, the less they interacted, the less fighting there was. She needed to find friends to go to their houses after school more often. She was in flight mode 24/7 now.

The more he was home, the more he drank. The amount of beer bottles started increasing. The number of times he opened a fresh beer was increasing. He had a routine she could hear from wherever she was in the house.

The sound of his 16 steps from the living room to the kitchen, the clink of putting an empty bottle in the empty six-pack container, then the fridge opening as he grabbed a fresh beer, the pop of the bottle cap, then the 16 steps back to the living room.

The more he was home and without his job, the more insecure he felt. Her mom kept working full time. He'd still yell and demand that someone bring him dinner, which would only light more of a fire in this little girl.

"Why don't you figure out your own dinner? You've been home all day," she'd say to him. Without knowing it, she hit on his insecurity even more. The fights between the father and the daughter increased.

At some point, he decided to take a solo trip around the world. What a relief this little girl felt! He was gone for months! There was peace in the house. Could this potentially be something that lasts longer than his planned trip? A girl could dream.

Looking back, it was also quite selfish of him to do. However, as a child, all she felt was relief, as if the clouds opened up to sunny skies. She doesn't quite remember the time frame of this. It all blurs together as the rest of her childhood does.

As an adult, when this girl's friends reminisce on their childhood and pick out specific memories, *happy* memories, they have a sense of nostalgia. All she can reminisce on is chaos.

She is so curious about this nostalgia others are lucky to have, she loves hearing these stories.

She never had laughter in her house. Sure, she sometimes laughed with her sister, or on the rare occasion she had friends over, there were laughs. But those memories others talk about when they sit around the table with extended family, laughing and telling stories? Nope. That is something she saw in other people's homes, in movies, in sitcoms. Something she had profound knowledge that she could create this joy in her own life one day.

The only part of her childhood that she felt a beaming sense of pride in herself, is that she always used her voice, and she always knew she needed to create her own path.

That path ahead wasn't well defined, but it did not need to be. It wasn't that she knew she wanted to be a doctor or a lawyer (actually, her father was a lawyer and she wasn't at all interested in following his path). Instead, she knew she needed to make a life for herself and create a *home* filled with peace. And laughter. And happy memories. The simplest of things had such a deep meaning to her.

She would create a home as she had only ever lived in houses after all, never a home.

She did not have time to think about what she wanted to be when she grew up because she was constantly in-flight mode. She was merely trying to get through the day and dreaming of the day she did not have to live under that roof.

At the time, she didn't realize it was flight mode. This was all simply *life*.

PART 2: FINDING SUCCESS ON AUTOPILOT

Those close to me would describe me as someone with drive, ambition, and relentless in the pursuit of success.

By my mid 30's, I had worked my way up in the startup world launching, scaling, and leading large organizations. Some of these startups have become household names.

I had made a career of building teams, processes, businesses that took messy operations, and made them more efficient. Throughout this I met amazing people, led teams of incredibly talented people. I ran towards the unsexy, complex, and tangled parts of a business and brought clarity and efficiency to them.

Yet, inside I had ignored the chaos in my nervous system, in my body. I thrived on *hyperfunctional autopilot.*

Hyperfunctional Autopilot
Operating in a constant "zoned out" state while moving through life in what looks like a successful, thriving way to others. It may seem intentional and aware from the outside, but deep within this is a state of achieving without much focus on the present and one's values nor the state of one's nervous system. An Energizer-bunny state-of-mind that first leads to professional success and often results in burnout.

After what felt like a lifetime and an instant all at once, I had spent over ten years building up my career and letting my life take a back seat.

Sure, I went on business trips and stayed in nice hotels, I ate at fabulous restaurants, I drank margaritas on beaches with girlfriends, I went on vacations to Aruba and Rome with my husband, but I also was neglecting my health, moving to cities I wasn't excited to live in (and dragging my supportive husband along with me), all while being tethered to my iPhone constantly checking work emails and Slack in case something urgent happened (and everything was urgent).

All decisions I consciously made while living in a state of *hyperfunctional autopilot*. All because I believed this is what was required to be successful, and to fully support myself in the world.

It turns out I lived my entire adult life operating in a constant state of *hyperfunctional autopilot*.

"How did I get here?" I would later wonder. And as I connected the dots, it was clear where my drive and ambition came from. The same thing that catapulted me to a successful career was the skill I developed as a young girl.

I lived my entire childhood in flight mode. That little girl, all of those experiences, those were all ME.

I'm the adult who was once that little girl, hoping her voice was heard, the little girl longing for laughter in her house, the little girl who always wanted to leave the house.

As an adult, I can look back and recognize the little girl was just stuck in flight mode and looking for an out, for a protective and supportive mother, for peace, for laughter.

On one hand, it's impressive that my childhood experiences shaped such positive characteristics in me. A woman with drive, persistence, and a strong voice are all great things. However, that very same *flight mode* I lived in as a child had transformed itself into *hyperfunctional autopilot* as an adult and I was missing balance and peace.

I knew I needed to start living for myself. I wasn't sure what that meant yet. But, being the driven and persistent person that I am, I knew I'd figure it out. Even if it took a few nudges from my body and wake up calls to figure it out, I knew I'd figure it out. I always did.

You see, being in *hyperfunctional autopilot* came so naturally to me yet it was also so stressful at the same time. My body had reminded me of that a few times—notably when I got shingles and traveled to a job interview despite that.

I woke up with huge, bright red welts on my back that burned, they must be bad spider bites, I thought. It was strange my husband did not have them though. I called a friend to catch up and showed her, immediately she pointed out that these were shingles. I did not even know what shingles were. I quickly looked it up: a virus usually caused by acute stress, not common in people under 60. I made an emergency doctor appointment the day before my flight to the job interview. The doctor quickly confirmed I had shingles, most likely my body's reaction to extreme stress. I picked up my antiviral prescription the night before I left for the airport for my interview the next day.

I did not think twice about the doctor's comment about how these were caused by stress. Was I stressed? Yes. Did I have the medicine and a job interview lined up to escape the stress of my current job? Also, yes. I wasn't focused on addressing the stress, instead I focused on my next steps. I did not have time to think about what caused them, I had an interview to focus on.

I packed, took an Uber to the airport, flew 3 hours to San Francisco, all while the hot shingles burned against the shirt on my back.

Luckily, the welts caused by shingles were only on my back and were easy to cover up, so I did what I needed to do to get through that interview. I planned a cute, professional outfit and sat down in a room I'd be in for the next 4+ hours despite my back being filled with shingles. The heat from the shingles was so intense it hurt when my shirt touched them and I couldn't lean against the chair, but I was determined to get through the interview and sat up straight as if nothing was wrong. After all, a woman running on *hyperfunctional autopilot* just keeps going, no matter what her body is telling her. That's exactly what I did.

And guess what? I killed the interview. But at what price?

Of course, I got that job. Of course, I did well at it. I'd go on to get promotions—more money and more titles even after the shingles interview.

Then I hit the point where this was no longer bearable.

Yet from the outside, you'd never know I needed this switch. When I was living in my *hyperfunctional autopilot* state, I did all the things—traveled, had great friends, went to happy hours, got promotions and new jobs at sexy companies—never for a minute looking like the overwhelmed, exhausted person I was on the inside.

But inside, my nervous system and mind needed to operate differently.

It came to a point where it was no longer bearable to keep living an unfulfilled and draining life.

We had finally moved to Miami—a place we loved and always wanted to be—and found a home in a neighborhood close to a big park on the bay. It was a dream. Working from home made it easier to move on our own, for our own happiness, and not because a job asked me to move.

I spent the move working—even though my boss and team knew we were driving a U-Haul across the country with all of our belongings, I made myself available for urgent work (and everything was urgent). I toggled my data from my phone to my laptop and had email, Slack, Google Sheets all open. I did it all from the passenger side of the U-Haul: updating a spreadsheet to pull reports, communicating an update in a process to the team, attending a leadership planning summit on Zoom, from the U-Haul. I could do this work and lead my team like the back of my hand.

Miami's sunshine, vibrant people, the *cafecitos* with friends, the palm trees, the walks along the bay, the beach—we were excited to finally be in a place we chose, a place that we loved waking up in.

As I filled our home with plants and decor—creating a home— and we started making friends in our new city, I realized there was still something not fully settled within me. My job was not only not fulfilling, it was becoming all consuming. I knew it was time to move on from my job. But, would I quit just to look for another job? Another job where I'd fall back into this cycle? Where I'd remain in *hyper functional autopilot*?

No, this time was different. I could feel it in my mind, body, and soul. I just knew I needed to take back my full life—and my job was the only thing still eating away at me.

This time, I did not get shingles (I mean, if I'm being honest when I got shingles, I did not stop for a minute to process what my body was telling me, I kept going, and remained on *hyperfunctional autopilot*).

Instead, this time I had an *aha* moment with myself.

This wasn't something I vocalized, nor was it something I really thought too long about. I realized that if a friend came to me in my position, I would advise them to make decisions for themselves. To break free of the empty jobs, to let go of the people pleasing to chase a career, and to focus solely on themselves. To finally fully enjoy the city I live in, and the life my husband and I dreamed of.

Break free. That's exactly what I sought: freedom of my own time. To spend it as I wished. To do things that I loved. To not be tethered to my iPhone and its constant notifications. To live this life the way I desired it.

I realized if I were to give this advice to a good friend, why wasn't I giving that advice to myself?

I knew it was time to start living for me, especially with how I worked. I needed to create a lifestyle free from *hyperfunctional autopilot* and job chasing, and climbing the career ladder. These were the last things holding me back from breaking free once and for all. How would I do that? I wasn't quite sure. But I knew the answer was not running to another job. Not this time.

At this point, I was a leader at the company and I had built a self-managing team in preparation of my departure. My *hyperfunctional autopilot* self was determined to leave the company and team in a much better place than I'd found it and I knew I'd done just that.

Once I decided to give notice and broke the news to leadership, they tried to get me to stay. A past-version of me (the version that gets shingles and still flies to job interviews) would have considered those options. I had planned a seamless, smooth resignation plan: a few calls to my boss and other leaders, alerting my direct reports, a team meeting, emails and documents outlining the transition plan, and a few months where I'd stay on to make sure everything was running smoothly as I transitioned out. The plan was solid. I thought it'd be a clean break, a straightforward exit.

My first call—my resignation call that should have been the first domino in my seamless plan—turned into a handful of follow-up calls with other leaders and a handful of conversations with HR, all trying to sell me on different visions and roles at the company. Just when I thought I could start clearing my calendar of meetings and letting my team know I'd be departing, my calendar was suddenly full of calls trying to get me to stay. These were *extra* calls on top of my existing meetings since I had to carry on my job as normal since my team and others did not know I'd planned to leave yet.

This felt even more chaotic than before I put in my notice and it wasn't leading to the change I wanted. It was the opposite of my plan. It was taking even more time away from me and I wasn't gaining anything from it.

I quickly declined their efforts to have me take on other roles and put an end to what seemed like never-ending follow-up calls to discuss my exit. I transitioned the conversations to negotiate an exit package and a plan that would allow me some time and freedom to contemplate what was next.

During this transition, I still thought that my next step might mean another job. Working for someone else, achieving their goals. I was good at it. And as far as I'd seen, that was the way you lived life. You work, maybe hit it big with a successful startup, cash in some options, get promotions, eventually retire. I just thought this time, I'd find some peace of mind and do it in a more sustainable way for me.

Little did I know a new path was being forged.

I felt immediate relief when I signed out of that job for the last time. The endless Slacks (still pinging away with the infamous Slack jingle on my way out), the urgent emails that kept pouring in even as I sent a final transition email. I closed the laptop for good, packed it up and sent it away. I was done. When I received the UPS box with the return label, I quickly put the laptop in, walked over to my local UPS, and sent the laptop away once and for all. On the way home, I took a long walk through the park along the bay near my house. A walk I intended to do daily when I moved to Miami, but work always got in the way.

This time, my shoulders were more relaxed, my jaw wasn't clenched, I people-watched, I listened to the different types of birds chirping, I saw dolphins swimming in the bay, sometimes I saw manatees. This is what I was missing. I was finally able to notice the world around me. This was my new normal.

The more I went on these walks, the freer my mind was. I finally had time to daydream about what I really wanted and needed without rushing into the next phase, or job.

PART 3: THE JOURNEY TO CONSISTENT EASE

As I went on my daily walks along the bay, sometimes stopping to sit and watch the sunrise over the bay, or sometimes to see the moon's reflection on the water, I started to think about working for myself.

Another new normal for me was heading to a local cafe on weekdays. Sometimes to enjoy a *cafecito* with my husband, sometimes with a book, and sometimes alone and with my computer to think about what was next for me.

I started thinking that working for myself was not too far off. Could I launch a consulting business? Many, many years back I casually said to a few coworkers, "What if we have our own consulting company and teach companies how to do this better?"

Little did I know, that comment I made was a manifestation the Universe planted on my path.

I decided I'd figure out a way to work that worked for me. No longer did I need to push my own boundaries to fit a company.

But at the time this seemed risky. Consulting was not a popular line of work (yet). It certainly wasn't trendy. It felt like I was going against the grain. Many thought I was crazy. After all, I had made a successful career leading operations of well-known tech companies. And now, I was going to throw away the job title and company logo on LinkedIn, the opportunity to work at yet another Unicorn startup (private companies valued at $1B or more are called Unicorns in the tech world and I've worked at a few), the hip office full of free snacks, and unlimited time off, just to go launch my own consulting agency?

Yet even knowing this, I wasn't keen to take the safe path. That would bring me right back to my old ways and I'd soon fall into *hyperfunctional autopilot* again. Plus, I'm a very driven person—something I can thank my younger self for—and when I set my mind to something I make it happen.

What if I could decide how I work? What if I worked for myself? What if I could work with a variety of companies, industries, and types of projects? And what if I could bring people into the work and build a business with me? That's what I loved doing anyways—building and developing teams, seeing something through from vision to strategy to execution, and working with all kinds of people and industries is really how I navigated my career, so why couldn't I do this on my own?

And most importantly, what if I could do this all while simultaneously focusing on other areas of life like hobbies, launching more than one company, making a doctor's appointment in the middle of the day without worrying about how it will affect my meetings, freedom of my time to daydream, going to a cafe during the week, going on my daily walks along the bay?

Once I made the decision, it all came together. I landed my first client within months and never looked back. The sense of freedom this gave me was immense.

There was another big shift I made in my life and mindset that took me to a new level during this time.

I decided to work on ME.

For so long, I was (and still am) the hype woman for my friends and colleagues. Friends who have a life update, big or small, know they can count on me to support and cheer them on. Whether it's launching new businesses, starting new jobs, starting a new hobby, or making a life change, I'm a proud hype woman.

I truly love cheering others on. But was I cheering myself on?

I decided to start working with a coach who could help me develop both as an executive and as a human.

I knew I needed someone in my corner to navigate this new season of life. Someone to support me, guide me. And help to make sense of all the choices, decisions I was making in my life. I needed someone from the outside to bring that calm and clarity that I sought. Someone to hold me accountable to staying on track to define and uphold my personal values that the *hyperfunctional autopilot* version of me was happy to disregard.

Many people call on their mom or dad to talk through decisions with—whether they be personal, professional, or to simply talk. That's not my reality. I had (and still have) great friends and a supportive husband, but I was seeking a figure to help me think through my values or big decisions from a more objective perspective.

I'd become so successful in my career and had built a life for myself where I relied on my own drive. I had escaped the flight mode and chaos that was my childhood and was so proud of that. But it wasn't until I took some planned time off of work that I thought deeply about how I did not have a "coach" in my corner. To change direction, I needed to have a new way of thinking. A coach would help hold me accountable, make value-aligned decisions, and help get me out of my own head.

It proved to be just what I needed.

Less than a year into launching my consulting business, I landed multiple clients, was making more money than ever before, was able to pay others I brought into projects, and was building a business. But you know what I also did? I went to my favorite cafes and sipped my latte slowly in the middle of the day. I started my morning on my balcony with a book as the sun rose. I went to the gym in the morning without checking emails. I took a six-week pottery class. All because I could organize my days in a way that worked best for me.

During this time, I also got a job offer. This job offer is something the previous version of myself would have loved! A true mission-driven startup, with a proven business model, doing work I personally could relate to and was passionate about. I was offered a generous VP package with a great salary, great perks. In fact, I had turned down previous executive offers before this offer because the companies or roles weren't aligned with my values—something that a previous version of me would have found difficult as I had a knack for validating why a yellow or red flag about a company was something I could help improve. Now, I had an offer in front of me that had no yellow or red flags.

But what about my own business? Was I really going to leave that behind? I was designing my own services, I was bringing folks into projects and building a team, I was building something I could scale. I also had the freedom to build quickly, slowly, or take on less work when I wanted to.

I was creating my own reality.

And I was loving how that felt.

No more anxiousness. No more stress. No more worrying about other people at the company, their expectations, their demands, none of it. This was all mine to create in a way that was fully aligned with the most authentic and truest version of me. Was I really going to leave that behind?

It was only six months since I left my last full-time job and began my entrepreneurial journey. In such a short time, I not only created my own new normal, I had also landed a dream role. How did both things happen so quickly?

My new reality was a dream. Time did not disappear into the overcrowded calendar blocks that used to fill my days. I would never again wake up and immediately check missed Slack messages, see what new emails came in since I last checked my email in bed less than eight hours before, go to the gym filled with anxiety about how long I'd be away from my Slack (even well before business hours), and get ready for eight hours of back-to-back zoom calls.

I was no longer living in a constant state of *hyperfunctional autopilot*. Instead, I was living in a state of calm and ease.

That did not make this decision easier. In fact, I was very excited about this role. I had presented a 3, 6, and 9 month vision to the team and was ready to execute on it. I had spoken with every executive team member, members of the team I'd potentially manage and gotten a great feeling from everyone. Maybe this would finally be the career move, the job, where I did not fall back into my old *hyperfunctional autopilot* patterns.

I had considered everyone else—the customers, the team, my would-be boss—but was I considering myself? Was I considering my needs, my desires, even my health? My own business I had launched? The reality I was creating? That turned out to be the biggest red flag with this job offer—the fact that I'd have to give all of that up.

When I got out of my head and considered a simple question my coach posed, it all became so clear. *How would I feel if my newly-signed client rescinded their contract? And then how would I feel if the company rescinded the job offer?* Immediately, I knew. I'd feel relieved if the company rescinded the job offer. I wouldn't have this decision to make! I'd be devastated if the new client rescinded their contract, but I'd continue building my business and land a few more clients soon.

It was so simple.

I knew there was more work to do building my business—first, as a solopreneur, later, building a team, and in the future, other ventures.

I made the tough call and turned down the role. I learned to say no to something that seemed so right for everyone else, but wasn't for me.

And what happened next was magical, the Universe had my back.

I continued working with the new client and signed in 2 more in a matter of months.

The more I focused on building the life I wanted, the more my business grew.

Through the next few years, I'd work with amazing clients on exciting projects all while living a life I loved.

There were some less than ideal clients sprinkled in there too. The path wasn't always linear. I made mistakes. And the old me popped through here and there. And when the old me showed up, so did my old friend, *hyperfunctional autopilot* reminding me I was veering away from what I was meant to be doing. But for the vast majority of my entrepreneurial journey, I am proud that I always found my way back to *me*. Not back to *flight mode* or *hyperfunctional autopilot*. But I found a way back to inner peace and calm, back to connecting with myself and the Universe. I found *consistent ease*.

Consistent Ease

The new state of mind I default to is neither flight mode nor hyperfunctional autopilot. Instead, consistent ease is about being in flow. Ease is not to be confused with easy. Rather it is a feeling that everything I'm doing—my work, how I spend my time, etc, brings a sense of inner peace. I now take on challenges, make decisions, and live daily based on what brings me a consistent sense of ease. It's intentionally consistent vs. constant as "constant ease" is not realistic. It's about consistency.

When *hyperfunctional autopilot* was my normal state of being, I was always rushing. Rushing daily to accomplish as much as I could. Rushing to get ready for meetings (replying to slacks and emails as I put on makeup, as I cooked). Rushing to a dinner or event with friends or my husband straight after my last meeting.

Rushing through the years to get promoted or to land the next role. Rushing to fit in vacations and create life memories. My life was constantly rushing around my work.

Rushing was normal and I was good at it. Rushing meant I stayed ready for what was next.

Now, I've created a reality where I'm free from rushing.

PART 4: TRUST IS THE ANTIDOTE

A previous version of me used to create so much separation between the little girl in flight mode, the woman I became who ran on hyperfunctional autopilot, and now to my state of consistent ease.

Now I realize they are all different versions of me that have now blended beautifully together.

I needed to escape my childhood realities, so I became a woman on a quest to create a life of my own, a life of success. As if career success validated my existence.

But now, I realize the little girl I knew and the woman I became were both looking for the same thing: calmness, clarity, to be surrounded by people who do what's right, and trust that I can guide myself to consistent ease.

Yet while I was stuck in flight mode and on hyperfunctional autopilot, my body survived on anxiety. Stress. Physical health issues (hello shingles).

But here's what I learned. The antidote to anxiety is not calm. It is trust.

Through work, I built these self-managing and successful teams not simply through hiring the right people, building the right processes, measuring the right data points, and innovation. The secret to the success was through the trust that those people, processes, and systems created.

It was in trusting myself where I would build the calm mind, I needed to be my healthiest, truest self.

Trusting that the little girl in me was taken care of. That she'd been through things she would never repeat with her own family. That she had created a home for herself, a home filled with laughter and memories. That these unfortunate events actually created a drive in her that is unique to her. And that little girl is what built the woman I am today.

I had separated the little girl from my adult self for so long. They were the same person genetically, but there was a clear line that separated them. When I grew up and began creating my own life, I left the little girl behind.

Yet, that boundary was in my head. I did not want to relate my current self to what the little girl had to endure. You can even sense it in the way this story is written—the little girl you meet is very intentionally written entirely in third person.

But that also meant I was pushing her out of my life when she is the very reason, I am who I am today.

I built an inner trust that the little girl—who had endured so much, had built a strong drive, and always recognized the strength of her voice—created the path to the woman I am.

Trying to create calm felt chaotic. Building the internal systems, practices, and dedicating time to myself (much like I had given to my teams and jobs) is what built the trust. The calm followed. I needed to build that version of a "self-managing" team in myself to achieve self-trust.

It takes time and trust to build consistent ease and calm. It required me to explore and address the innermost parts of me, the parts that make me who I am, especially the parts that are fueled by trauma and unpleasant experiences.

It also required me to acknowledge and accept that I am the only one who can use the fullest version of myself, including all versions of me from the past, to motivate myself in spite of what the little girl in me had to endure. I turned chaos into drive and ease.

It is through trust in myself and accepting and trusting the little girl I once was, that I have developed the antidote to anxiety and stress.

Trust is the antidote.

Kelly thrives on bringing ideas and projects to life, with writing being her latest endeavor. She has a talent and passion for creating ease, clarity, and momentum for those around her—personally and professionally.

Professionally, her expertise lies in scaling teams, leadership development, and driving alignment. Over the first 15 years of her career, Kelly played a key role in developing and scaling operations teams at household-name companies like Airbnb and Uber.

Today, Kelly helps leaders build their businesses through Business Rhythms, her proprietary framework is to set goals, align teams, and achieve exceptional results. In addition, she is the co-founder of Kairos Studio, a business strategy and leadership development studio specializing in scaling customer operations. She lives with her husband in beautiful Miami, where she enjoys pottery, plants, and afternoon cafecitos. Connect with Kelly on LinkedIn at kelly-feeney or visit her website at kellyfeeney.com.

Falling Into My Life

BY MANDY MCLAUGHLIN

Imagine looking through the French doors of my sunroom on a cold winter night to see my beautifully decorated home with five perfectly decorated Christmas trees. Yes, five! It was the end of January and the trees were still up. It was driving me crazy for a while but, to be honest, I was avoiding it. I was just completely exhausted. Instead of taking down the decorations, I was in my bath, candles glowing, water in a fancy wine glass, listening to a beautiful meditation on energy. I was romanticizing my life with subtle little changes. It was something I learned from the new personal growth academy I just joined. I was inspired to get control of my life.

"You got this, Mandy," I said to myself. I finished my bath and put on a clean, soft nightgown. I went downstairs, put on some music and went to where the first tree was in the corner of my sunroom. As I was taking off ornaments, staring at the tree all lit up, I remembered the joy I felt decorating and choosing the theme for this tree. I made it for my husband hoping that he would love it. It was a "male" themed Christmas tree, decked out with red and black buffalo patterned ribbon, old vintage truck ornaments, deer antlers and a burlap bow on the top. I loved it and was hoping it would catch his attention, but it never did, really. It was hard enough for me to catch his attention, let alone a Christmas tree.

As I continued to take each ornament off the tree, I remember feeling the best I had felt in a while. "Mandy, you are doing so good," I caught myself saying out loud. I was finally getting my life together after being separated from my high school sweetheart of 25 years. He left me two times in the last five years. Yes, two times. Both times I went crashing down with the deepest heartache I had ever experienced. I was depressed but I was hiding it. I was stuck in a fantasy of a dream life I wanted with him since I was sixteen. Ask me honestly if I was happy those last five years? If I was in love, truthfully. The answer was absolutely not. I was in habit, not in love. Doing the same thing every day, hoping to build a healthy marriage with the man that used to be my best friend. Trying my best not to be extremely jealous of all the people that occupied his time. But was I ever brave enough to leave? No, not in a million years. I would have stayed unhappy my whole life at that point. I now know why. I did not love myself enough.

He wasn't happy and I could see it. He didn't love himself and seemed completely lost, unsure of what he wanted. Worst of all, he hated coming home. He hated being inside the house. Many times, he reminded me that everything was bothering him, from what I chose to wear, to my makeup, to me speaking when he did not want me to. All of it was too much for him. I wish I had a voice back then. I would have spoken up. I would have said, "I like our house. I like what I wear. I like my makeup too."

But I kept quiet, believing I was the problem and that he was right. His work life was chaotic, and years of not loving himself led to even more chaos. I knew all of this and yet, I felt like a magnet being pulled into his storm. I was scared of the tornado coming home. I never knew what personality would walk through that door. Did he have a good day or a bad day? Shouldn't I be patient and understanding? He worked so hard for us after all.

It was a great deal of mistreatment and it deeply affected me emotionally. Even now, all these years later, I hate admitting it. I did not fully understand how bad things were back then. I just thought he was unhappy and it was my responsibility to fix that. I was hoping maybe it would get better if I just kept everything perfect—the house, the kids, and myself as the perfect wife always trying to be thinner, more attentive and more understanding.

My therapist taught me the story of the River of the Tao during one of our sessions. He helped me see I wasn't going with the "flow of the river." Instead, I was running upstream against the current. I didn't want to believe it, but deep down, I knew it was true. I felt it every day in my bones. I was living in survival mode. The last few years of our marriage, I was actively ignoring every single feeling I was having. Then I read these words by Bob Proctor that changed everything, "You can't escape a jail If you don't know you're in one."

I was in denial jail.

Even after my husband left me for the second time, I denied what was happening. I was stuck. I was stuck in fake land not wanting anyone to know. I felt like a failure as a wife and the rejection was so hard to go through even though I knew in my heart this was happening for me.

Once when we were on a vacation, I remember thinking, "Wow, he doesn't want me here." Everything I did was wrong. He had so much anger towards me for no reason. I was so upset in our hotel room I went in the shower and cried. *"I can't do this anymore,"* I thought, *"the bullying was too much and our son was getting it too."* I remember I texted my therapist, "This is it! I am done."

Suddenly, there was a knock on the bathroom door. He stood there and said, "Give me a kiss," and I did. I let it go again, thinking he must love me and this was going to get better. Three days later, the day we got back home from our trip, he left again. He was honest and told me he was not happy. He was not in love with me and he was done for good. He told me he will always take care of me, and love me more than I will ever know.

Rejection equals God's protection and redirection. It was the biggest sign the Universe was giving me. I was being rejected over and over again. But I wasn't listening. I had many people tell me, even my doctor who I called crying the afternoon when my husband left me the second time, "Mandy, welcome to the first day of your fucking life."

I remember wondering, "Really? Could this pain and sadness actually be the start of something?" Through my fearful tears, I actually had it in me to smile a little.

My children came into my room and sat on the bed with me. I let them know that he left. He left in a black car for the airport to Germany.

My kids were truly happy it was over. "Did he really leave for good Mom?" my daughter asked.

"*Yes*, it's over for good," I promised.

"Mom I am so done with you living your life for Dad. It is time to live your life for you." My kids cheered me on to finally live my life to the fullest. They were then, and continue to be, the most amazing and supportive part of my life.

I knew it was over, but I was still holding onto this fear of being independent. I really had not done anything for myself. I had been riding his coattails, fearing failure, fearing the uncertainty of navigating a divorce, and fearing what others may think. My self confidence was extremely low. I had huge doubts about myself and no idea what I wanted in life. I was truly living for him and the kids. Deep down, I knew I deserved more love and attention, but I kept trying to people please my way through life. For so long, I sought validation from outside myself, doing my best to please others, not really to please them, but to hope they like me.

Living my best life? That was the last thing I was doing. Heck, I had no idea what my best life even looked like. All I wanted in life was to be the perfect wife to him which meant don't complain, don't ask for time with him and just kept hoping there would be this miracle that he would finally see me and want to have quality time with me. But even as I hoped for a miracle, I knew he didn't love me.

The question I should have been asking myself was, "Do I love me?" Never once did I put the love into me that I wanted him to put into me. I simply did not love me. As I have grown through these moments going inward, finally listening to me, listening to the Universe, listening to the nudges, I realize I am enough. I am more than enough to love. I am blessed. The Universe was talking so sweetly to me more and more each day. They are not just empty affirmations that I say robotically. They are words that truly reflect how I feel about me. But getting here took time.

Little by little I became grateful for this shift in my life. Being able to get out of bed was my big win some days. I learned to put one foot down after another and say thank you. I am grateful for each step I took to reprogram Mandy.

I started to ask myself "Who am I?" I had to really think about it. Firstly, I am a determined super woman with two beautiful children, my proudest accomplishment. I always knew I was the best at being a mom. I have the best friends a girl could ever ask for and a supportive family. My kids, my friends, my family, everyone could see my true power but me.

All of these thoughts were floating in my mind as I got to the top of the Christmas tree to remove the burlap bow. I pulled a chair from my oak dining table and put it up against the hutch. Then, for some reason, I thought it was a good idea for me, forty years old, to climb on top of it and reach for the bow. As I stretched my hand to reach for the bow while perched awkwardly on the hutch, I fell off the hutch and onto the chair. The chair broke. I landed on the cold unforgiving tile. I hit my head. I hit my wrist. I hit my foot. To top it off, I landed in a puddle of dog piss that my dog left while I was not looking.

I knew I broke something. I was in so much pain. But what truly shattered in that moment was something deep within me.

"I need help."

My hair was wet with pee. The pain inside of me exploded. It was like an egg cracked in me, pouring out the most rage I had ever felt. Tears streamed down my face. Everything I was holding in just came out of me. I screamed out loud.

"I NEED FUCKING HELP."

Pain, that relentless teacher, had me cornered. The Universe was no longer whispering, it was screaming, demanding my attention. No more tiptoeing around your own life! I remember yelling into the pain and in those moments surrendered.

"I am done! I need more help! And how is this my fucking life? And why am I ok with this?!"

I crawled to my phone which was in the living room and called my parents. My father answered and came rushing to my side.

When my dad arrived, he told me, "Honey, I think you broke your arm and your foot." But even then, I was in denial.

My dad has always been and always will be my hero. He taught me so much throughout my life. He had continued to watch me be sad and would say, "Honey, shake it off like the Taylor Swift song." He would remind me of my power and many times question, where was fairness in all this. One day he was helping me at the spa and wellness centre that I owned. I asked him to help me with my books and see why I wasn't doing as well as I felt I should be. He came into my office and he showed me my numbers. "Mandy, it's simple. You are giving everyone more than half of what you are putting in. Where is the fairness in these numbers?" When he said the word "fair" something finally clicked. It was a Soul Spark.

The Universe was saying he was right, you deserve more. I was able to lead my staff and tenants better after that day. He helped my self-worth with that advice and I could feel it in everything I did from that day on.

The next morning, I went to the hospital. I had been working from my bed and I could not even pick up my pen. One of my best friends came over to see me and she convinced me to finally go. I drove myself, still not accepting help. I got a beautiful pink cast on my arm and refused to cast my foot (too stubborn).

Laying in the hospital bed, I knew that my life had to change. I was so focused on receiving love from the one person who clearly didn't have it in him to give it to me, so much so that I didn't see all the love that was pouring out of me. My dream was to help others find their inner warrior the more I found mine. I wanted to help other women, but I was not taking my own advice. I was preaching it, but I wasn't practicing it enough. I was seeing the sparks but not living by them. That day I made the intention to start listening to the Universe, accept help, and get the support I needed to be the best version of Mandy. I once read, "Small keys still open big doors." If only I could just do a little better each day and trust what I was learning from my mentors life would get better.

But it first required letting go of my inner roommate. That voice in my head. She was still trying to take me down with negative thoughts about myself.

Picture her like the roommate who has her stuff everywhere. She is rude, messy, loud, and has no sense of respect. That voice lived inside me. She wasn't kind to me at all. In some ways, my inner roommate was worse than my ex.

She was holding me back from loving my life. Not encouraging me. She was a total bitch. She was mean when I looked in the mirror at myself. She made me feel fat, ugly, not important, dumb, stupid, not successful. You name it. She spewed the hurt and I believed everything she said. My inner roommate was shooting these words at me all the time. She was the head of the "itty bitty shitty committee," as my yoga instructor once called it.

It is remarkable how a moment of such vulnerability can spark such profound clarity. I was confined to a hospital bed, and still could reprogram myself, my thinking. It did not happen overnight, but over time, I started to really cancel out my inner roommate. The more I read self-help books, watched YouTube videos, and wrote journal prompts onto little sticky notes and posted them all over the house, the more I realized, I am a superwoman. I am a warrior.

A new voice began to spark saying, "*own it, Mandy. Everything works out for you Mandy.*"

I put these words on sticky notes, and I started to live by these words. I played uplifting music all day and allowed these words to integrate into all of me. Best of all, I discovered the secret to finding my courage and building confidence. It was being surrounded by a supportive, encouraging, uplifting community. When I would doubt myself, I knew I could borrow other people's belief in me. My faith soared as I continued to nurture and love up Mandy. With each passing day, I uncovered new depths, new facets of her being, and my love grew stronger. I was rewriting her story, reclaiming her power, and the Universe had my back, I felt it. I was learning who Mandy was. I was reprogramming her, and I was truly falling in love with her.

This profound faith and belief in me wasn't always easy. But it's in the moments when you're down that you gather this warrior strength and dig deep down. Yes, it takes all the guts to try, but you go anyway, feeling like shit. You show up. Show up to work, show up for your family, you go to that work out when you don't feel like it. That faith in your inner self, that is where miracles are born in this state.

I am proof. I reprogrammed my inner roommate. I started really studying my inner self every day. I went to therapy to awaken my thoughts. I was believing in myself. I was meditating, going to yoga regularly, even with the cast on. I was starting to be Mandy 4.0. The old Mandy would wake up and not want to move. Now, when I wake up my inner roommate says "Good morning! You are a rock star! I laughed when I realized my inner roommate's new voice, "Wow, I sure am growing." The reprogramming was me, reminding myself each day: *Mandy believes a miracle is going to happen.*

Now she is always reminding me all is well. Taking the steering wheel of life and going for it all. Reprogramming our beliefs can be really fun too. I quote Bob Proctor a lot because he really saved my life. He would say, repeat these new affirmations of Mandy. Want to be more? Tell yourself you already are. And the more you do, you will start to believe it is possible. He's funny. He said even if it feels like you're lying to yourself, you'll eventually start to believe it. I did exactly what he taught. And guess what? It worked. I can now emotionally regulate myself like a thermostat and turn fear into faith and always return to love. I have never felt more powerful.

As I studied more and more about myself in my courses, I felt mentally stronger each and every day. One day, about 6 months after we separated, my daughter received a very emotionally upsetting phone call from a stranger. Boy did it take us by storm. We were in the car together when she said "Mom, this number keeps calling me." I told her to answer it, reassuring her that it was okay because I was there. Let's just say parts of the tornado that I was living through in the past came flying through that phone. Information about my ex was revealed. I felt sick to my stomach. The call was horrible. But even in that gut wrenching moment, I realized that the Universe did not provide me with this information until I was ready. The Universe always had my back.

At that moment, I realized how delusional I was in the past. Some days, as I was healing and getting stronger mentally, I would just think about going back to the way it was. It was me not wanting to grow as the growing pains sucked. But after that call, I knew I had to go through it to grow from it. When I told my Dad about the phone call he said "this is great news! Finally, the nails are in the casket."

I did feel a sense of relief too after the news settled. Mostly, I was relieved at how strong I was becoming. Even my daughter felt it. I realized; everything is happening at the perfect time. Let go. Trust the process and with ease and grace.

And trust me when I say, that is a far cry from the woman I once was.

I started listening and seeing signs everywhere. Signs that the Universe is always working in our favor, working for us, supporting us.

From a bird feeder, to the oven pre-heat timer, to lighting a match to an Amazon truck. Everything was speaking to me and saying, "Hello Mandy! Listen up!" All of it was me stepping into the truest version of me.

THE BIRDFEEDER

As I was studying in my office, I caught myself gazing out of my window. My father had placed a bird feeder outside my window so I could watch them. He knew how much I love them. I was now an empty nester and bird watcher. As I stared out the window, a big blackbird appeared. I thought it was a crow and it was bullying all my other beautiful birds, the doves, cardinals, blue jays, and finches.

I let my Dad know that this was happening. I thought there has to be some type of birdseed that I could get that would get that bully bird to go away.

It had been a few weeks and when my dad came into my office, he said to me, "Have you noticed that the bully bird is gone?"

I said to my dad, "Yes actually, I did notice! I've been seeing some of the other birds again. What kind of magnificent special birdseed did you buy?"

He looked at me and he said, "Mandy, I didn't buy any special birdseed. I stopped feeding the birds."

The birds were there to teach me a really big lesson. I liked to overthink everything and believed everything needed my special help when it could actually be really simple. "All we need to do is stop feeding them, and they will go away," my Dad told me,

"If they come back, well, stop feeding them again." They would just go and find a new place to eat. That's when I realized, not everything needed my special help.

It was time to stop feeding the birds and let them discover their own wings. I did not have to find a solution to everything. I didn't have to solve every problem. Instead, I could just stop feeding the birds. It was a Soul Spark. The Universe was whispering "Let it be easy, Mandy," Stop giving thoughts, emotions, and situations. Stop feeding the birds. Just let it be easy.

PRE-HEAT TIMER

One morning, I was feeling a little stuck. I just had a feeling that the day would drag. Lucky for me, I had an emotional toolbox I carried around full of ways to help me when I felt stuck. So, I played Mandy's manifestation playlist that I created to help me in these moments. Music was one of my favorite tools, second only to meditation. This morning I knew I just needed 5 minutes of quiet and I would feel better. I sat in my favorite yellow comfy chair, I closed my eyes, set a timer for five minutes, and surrendered to the quiet. I was still deep in my thoughts breathing rhythmically when the five minutes were up. I thought, "*Wow, Mandy that was fast! I did not get anything in that time.*" But then, the preheat timer went off on my oven. I remembered that I had made a quiche that morning. The Universe was speaking to me, telling me, "*You are in preheat mode Mandy. It is ok, your goals are taking some time. You are warming up.*"

If I would have put the quiche in the oven without the preheat timer, it probably wouldn't have been as cooked and delicious. It was just like me. I need to warm up, do the work, recharge to be the most fabulous version of me!

This was way better than the time I put the quiche in the oven, walked out to my barn to clean and completely forgot about the quiche and burnt it to a crisp! I took that as a sign to not forget about myself. Otherwise, I will burn out like the quiche! As my friend Eric Bigger says, "Never rush your greatness because your timing has a purpose."

See all the ways the Universe was speaking to me? All the messages are just popping into my everyday life. I loved receiving each one. The Universe kept giving me signs, it was up to me to follow them.

Almost two years after I fell from that Christmas tree and landed in dog pee, I am writing this chapter immersed in the ambiance of the most enchanting cafe in Paris all by myself. For the first time in my life, I am on a 21-day trip through Europe with a friend. Sitting here sipping my latte, I know I have come a long way. It is such a full circle moment, being in this cafe in Paris, just watching the world go by. I caught myself staring at a couple holding hands, seeing their love and knowing that someday, everything would work out for me. I will find my new love as I find myself. My inner roommate came to Paris too! I heard her saying "Wow! This is your fucking life!" Sure is, Mandy. I saw myself at the bottom of the Christmas tree, bawling, in the most agonizing pain, to the most amazing feeling of accomplishment.

I immediately texted my friend and publisher what I was doing, where I was and the realization that was coming through. She replied, "You should call your chapter, From dog piss to Paris!" Boy, ain't that the truth.

Every setback in my entire life has been a set up for me to be better.

I am grateful to have ended my marriage. To cultivate a much more respectful and amicable relationship with my children's father. I learned to let all the resentment go and instead, pour all the love into myself. As I embraced self-love, it not only transformed me, but also inspired him to treat me—and others— with love and respect. Now my children's father almost every day thanks me for being such an amazing mother to our kids and expresses how grateful he is. All because I loved myself and created a powerful ripple effect.

That fall cracked the shell of my former self, and from it emerged a stronger, more vibrant spirit—a woman who embraces her femininity, pursues her goals with passion, and radiates faith and love. Without the pain I would have never become who I am today. Challenges are opportunities. Thank them and always remember: I am worth committing to because I know my value and I refuse to settle for less than I deserve.

I am worth appreciating.

I am worth loving.

I am worth taking chances.

I am worth whatever my heart desires.

There are no limits for Mandy. Let me tell you, you are reading these words because it is true for you too.

As my mentor says "There is only one moment and one time to become the best of yourself and that is right now!" —Kathleen Cameron

Let today be the first day of your fucking life.

With love,
Mandy and the Universe

Mandy McLaughlin, a proud mother of two—Tommy and Evelyn—lives on a beautiful farm in a small town of Tillsonburg, Ontario, Canada. She is the visionary owner of Spa Marché, a spa and wellness center that goes beyond traditional services by integrating multiple therapy rooms and online virtual mentoring to embody beauty from the inside out. This is the second book Mandy has contributed to, reflecting her deep passion for growth and personal development. Currently advancing her studies in manifestation, leadership, marketing, and business consulting, Mandy is dedicated to helping others discover and embrace the best version of themselves.

SCAN HERE TO
LEARN MORE ABOUT